ESOTERIC AND MYSTICAL EXPERIENCES
OF MASTER NIKOLAOS A. MARGIORIS

SUPERVISION OF THE WORK
This work has been edited by the following persons:
Ilias L. Katsiampas
Vana L. Katsiampas
Lamprini Sp. Polizois
Translation editor: Anatolie Fitopoulou

Cover: Mediterra Books
Production supervisor: Platon Malliagkas – mediterrabooks.com

OMAKOIO OF TRIKALA
METAPHYSICAL STUDIES IN YOGA & SHIATSU
21 KEFALLINIAS STREET, 42131 TRIKALA, GREECE
Tel. no.: 0030-24310-75505 or 0030-6974-580768,
Websites: http://www.omakoio.gr or https://omakoio.blogspot.com
E-mails: omakoio@omakoio.gr or omakoeio@gmail.com
© ILIAS L. KATSIAMPAS
«ESOTERIC AND MYSTICAL EXPERIENCES
OF MASTER NIKOLAOS A. MARGIORIS»
FIRST BILINGUAL EDITION (GREEK - ENGLISH)
A PHOTOCOPIED STUDY IN PRINTED FORMAT
TRIKALA 2004, GREECE

FIRST (SECOND) ENGLISH EDITION 2016
«ESOTERIC AND MYSTICAL EXPERIENCES
OF MASTER NIKOLAOS A. MARGIORIS»
TRIKALA, GREECE

© 2016 ILIAS KATSIAMPAS

ISBN: 978-618-82675-1-0

ILIAS L. KATSIAMPAS

ESOTERICISM FOR ALL

ESOTERIC AND MYSTICAL EXPERIENCES

OF MASTER NIKOLAOS A. MARGIORIS

The collection and transcription of esoteric and mystical experiences
of Nikolaos A. Margioris, the modern Greek spiritual Master and Mystic,
who wrote 180 occultist and mystical works

OMAKOIO OF TRIKALA,
FIRST ENGLISH EDITION, 2016

CONTENTS OF THE ESSAY
ESOTERIC AND MYSTICAL EXPERIENCES
OF MASTER NIKOLAOS A. MARGIORIS

INTRODUCTION

After many years of thorough research, investigation and study, we discovered that there is a big void concerning the transcription of small or great esoteric experiences of spiritual Masters.

And this void is more apparent when we refer to the **revelatory works** that touch upon the **mystical truth** and its rendition in **physical form** (oral and particularly written).

In view of the fact that existing written records of spiritual experiences are few, extremely terse, hard to understand or unconnected with each other – and for the most part of little esoteric or spiritual depth – we thought that it would be useful to provide examples of **spiritual occurrences** found in the **hyperconscious experiences** of our Master **Nikolaos A. Margioris** that concern all of humanity and the course of its evolution which, through its gradual self-perfection, is ultimately guided towards them.

Because descriptions of such **profound spiritual experiences** (apart from or along with the presence of occult experiences) are few and far between, especially those accompanied by a rich analysis and an extensive unrivalled description, we deemed it imperative to collect them and to record them for everyone's benefit.

Additionally, it is with certainty that we believe that prominence can and should be given, whenever possible, to the **unwavering STANDARDS leading** towards the **ONE hyperconscious path of ascension** and **true spiritual ENLIGHTENMENT** as well as to the everlasting **qualities of THEOSIS** which may be detected or at least mentioned. Because of this certainty, we make these highly valuable and interesting spiritual experiences public for the first time.

In this way, one can be directly informed from the testimonial records of the experiences of the **Great Spiritual Masters** and to raise the standards of his ability to make spiritual distinctions, to consistently and with certainty distinguish between the perfect fruit of the spirit and the transient ones that surround us and go by various names. They pressure us in the name of the spirit, seeking to exacerbate our alienation and accelerate our fall into matter.

We believe that there are two main reasons for the scarcity of records of spiritual experiences; save for some very specific exceptions, of course, which are not always of the highest standards.

The **first cause** is the very few instances of real **spiritual Masters on a mission** being present and the scarcity of oral testimonies that they have confided in their students, and even fewer written records of their words.

Of course, it may be due to the fear that our fellow beings may touch that which is sacred, thus defiling and "degrading" the nature of such a pure experience, or use it for their own benefit. Or perhaps it may be due to the knowledge that there is an immense range of gradations and qualities of esoteric and spiritual experiences among the Masters and the Avatars, from the lowest to the highest, that may create problems (and confusion) for the seeker and the student instead of resolving them. Perhaps it is simply due to the objective inability of the human mind to conceive the inconceivable by any physical means even if they are within the restricted place-time limits that constrain us unbearably. It may be due to the karmic suitability or unsuitability of the times we are traversing or the foresight of the Divine Plan for each age. Finally, it could be a result of some of the above or a combination of all the aforementioned.

The **second cause** concerns the timidity and cowardice (inexperience-immaturity) often displayed by the students–staff of the Masters, who, in the name of a misunderstood preservation of the truth, attempt to "withhold" the experiences of their Masters, guarding them for themselves or for their inner circle. Some even place this knowledge on a high pedestal accessible only to those whom they deem worthy recipients of such information after they have seriously studied, applied, familiarized themselves with and grasped the basic esoteric truths that give value and meaning to the earnest search for spiritual experiences.

Undoubtedly, the distinction and the gradual revelation of esoteric details to the newly initiated should always exist. However, when we have in our hands the experiences that the Masters themselves wrote down in books or their oral testimonies that were later transcribed, it is foolish

– if not an indecency against truth and the Masters – if we don't make them public.

And this is because a spiritual experience that an illuminated being has, whether we realize it or not, concerns each of us separately and it also becomes our own experience. It belongs to us, **it belongs to all of humanity for which it was given** and not solely to the individual that experienced it.

The secrecy that prevails in certain circles and the "shrouding" of spiritual experiences, which in essence are given by God to one of His exquisite children for all of humanity, irrespective of whether they are accepted or experienced by all, is a fundamental mistake, a criminal act.

They constitute the glow of **Divine Grace** that everyone without exception may bask in and consult and feel something "breaking" within them. Thus, spiritual experiences must never be hidden or marginalized because they have been given by **God** for the **ENLIGHTENMENT** of every one of His human children and they serve this purpose exactly.

Those who keep them obstinately for themselves commit the greatest karmic error and they will surely receive punishment for their action.

There are many types–levels of spiritual experiences, which, however, we cannot include in the present work that focuses only on noting down the significant esoteric and spiritual experiences of Nikolaos A. Margioris.

Perhaps in other writings in the future, we will be given the opportunity to examine more thoroughly many of these types, to proceed as much as possible with the necessary distinctions and basic classifications in order to better perceive esoteric reality rising like the sun–the light before us.

The present essay, as well as the other works of the Umakoio of Trikala, has been translated into the English language in order that many of the Greek diaspora or of our foreign fellow beings who don't speak the Greek language well may benefit from such information and the knowledge provided.

PREFACE

When our Master **Nikolaos A. Margioris** was still with us, he himself gave us permission to teach his work as well as to disseminate every confidence that he delivered to us. And so, we consider it our moral obligation to make some of his written work known as well as a few of his oral testimonies, which we have gathered and classified. We do this because we **firmly** believe that the **Esoteric Truth**, or even certain aspects of it, need to come to the "foreground" because it may – despite difficulties understanding it and some of the ideological differentiations – provide interesting and important stimuli and may guide more of our fellow beings if not to the conquest of the same or similar experiences, at least to a **profound consideration** of **Life** and of the **Mysteries** that it contains, and they may find themselves better informed and willing to undertake, with greater sensitivity and understanding, the responsibilities that correspond to the course of their individual evolution as well as their collective evolution, as humanity.

We point out that the Experiences that follow must not be seen within a narrow dogmatic context, according to stereotypes and based on narrow anthropomorphic perceptions. Only in this way will the interested individual be able to probe deeper into the meanings they contain without distractions and with a clear mind.

This means that a restless soul who sees things with an esoteric, probing and detached eye will be able to benefit to the maximum without cringing at these new forms of expression or elements that seem 'odd' or paradoxical and, at first sight, may sometimes not appear to be absolutely clear and straightforward. Besides, we got a very good taste of the 'oddities' of Creation in the most emphatic way with the revelations of Quantum Physics as well as with those of Cosmology.

At no point did we change the style and the way the texts were conveyed; we only allowed ourselves to do some very basic editing, without changing the content and fully respecting the vibrational expression of our Master's description of his experiences, which we faithfully reproduced.

We recommend you study the text carefully and with an open mind, without rushing to conclusions, and to retain the stimuli that may not be comprehensible today for the future when, with the weight of the additional knowledge you will acquire, it may become clearer, allowing you to comprehend the manifold complexity of the described experience.

We hope this book proves beneficial and fruitful for all of our readers.

DESCRIPTION OF THE FIRST SPIRITUAL EXPERIENCE
OF MASTER NIKOLAOS A. MARGIORIS (1913-1993)

(As transcribed in the epilogue of his book, *Raja Yoga. Noetic Elevation of the Mind from Consciousness to Hyperconsciousness.*)

Transcription – Editing: **Ilias L. Katsiampas**
Nikolaos A. Margioris' *student*
Head of the **Omakoios** *of* **Trikala**
and **Thessaloniki**

Clarification: The Experience that appears below concerns **Nikolaos A. Margioris (1913-1933)**, who, in the epilogue of his book **Raja Yoga. Noetic Elevation of the Mind from Consciousness to Hyperconsciousness"**, for educational and informative reasons, describes the first **spiritual Experience–Samadhi–Theosis** that he had at a young age (almost 13 years old) as well as **antecedent events** that took place during his childhood and led him to this full **Experience–Enlightenment.**

With a view to informing all interested seekers or students of **Esotericism**, we quote the experience of N. Margioris unaltered, as he himself wrote it down, highlighting the points that we consider of primary importance and deserving of special attention in bold characters or upper case or underlined.

DESCRIPTION OF MASTER NIKOLAOS A. MARGIORIS' FIRST SPIRITUAL EXPERIENCE

In this part of this scientific book on **RAJA YOGA**, in the epilogue, I shall talk to you about what I didn't manage to write as I was developing the chapters. And that because it is irrelevant in depth and something separate.

It concerns experiences of the writer on the subject I am writing about and the narration of these experiences takes place in order to help the reader to judge as much the **written account** as well as his own possible **impulses** for the **Mysteries** of our **Being**.

When I was very young, almost a child, a very young child, I felt within me the **unbridled desire** to look beyond the world that the senses brought before me. This was something **particularly Vital** that bubbled inside me and dictated that I conform to its demands. **Images** unrelated to my childhood interests flew before me, in **my wake** and in my **daily life**, like **otherworldly memories** and **faded dreams**.

It didn't happen only once or twice that, as I was sitting, trying to sort out and classify these memories, I felt my head becoming heavy and the limbs of my body going numb. My eyes would then close and I saw that I was flying in other worlds, searching for the **Passage**. I had a **strange sensation** about IT then. As if it were a **Special Passage**, through which I would pass and find myself in other completely **different Worlds**, where instead of childish games, I would see **Sages** who would teach me incomprehensible things.

With these premature thoughts about life or about another different life, I travelled through the worlds of my childhood – perhaps – imagination until one time, I found myself before this **Torrent** of **strange Light** that came from a strange **HOLE** as big as the **Sky** – always according to my childhood imagination.

A gravitational force took hold of me and brought me, little by little, closer to this **Extraordinary Fire**, through or around which some **odd beings**, quite different to those I knew, passed. But the strange thing was that the more I approached this strange passageway, this **colourless Fire**, this smokeless and heatless fire, I didn't feel the Fire burning me or even scaring me.

In fact, at one point, I seemed to remember that I had passed through this region of the **Luminous Beam**, and, in fact, I remembered that I had not been alone but accompanied by many of my folk, and actually those very close to me. Then I looked around me, but, this time, on this journey of mine near the **Luminous Passageway**, I saw nobody but nobody accompanying me. I was momentarily taken aback. But then I comforted myself by telling myself that others would come to help me.

So, I again set myself free, getting closer and closer to the **Vast Passageway** and trying to approach as much as I could the parts that looked somewhat familiar from my past ascensions, to get to the **Unknown**. At exactly that moment, I realized that I wasn't alone. An **otherworldly**,

Crystal-Clear Voice was guiding me every step of the way and was specifying the places where I would pass in order to enter exactly the same Luminous Ray, from which I had passed at some point.

But as it were, the voice was drawing nearer and I recognized it. I began to dance, and I too began to call out its name, the name of the Entity, in its existent or non-existent form, that in a strange but familiar, beloved, unforgettable and Eternal Voice was summoning me to approach, using another one of my favourite names.

Following this voice, I came nearer and nearer to the now Luminous Sky, which was forming and reforming before the strange lights I was looking at when I felt myself being carried away by a great Wave of Attraction, a feeling exactly like the one I had when I first swam in the sea.

At that moment, I lost all sense of the world around me. Everything was suddenly lost, as was I.

In a matter of seconds, I found myself high above, at the place where I remembered being before I ascended and before I penetrated the Circle, The Ring Pass Not (not beyond the ring of rationalism). But with my abrupt passage through the Central Torrent of Fire and the momentary loss of my perception of events around me, I felt something extraordinary, something very difficult to explain and to interpret, something that cannot be said alone and a strong Mind can bear and ABOVE ALL grasp.

A strange and unfamiliar and incomprehensible

sensation-perception possessed me now. Within me, EVERYTHING was lost, completely lost and only ONE thing remained.

I thought and I felt that the ENTIRE world bonded with me and I with It, and that now I had supposedly found my correct state, that of the whole of Creation becoming ONE with me.

In the beginning, this type of sensation-perception was a sharp and painful pinch. I became agitated. Looking down in my room, I saw my physical body, as if in a Vision, lying there, very very small, and I didn't like it at all. It did not at all tally with what I was feeling at that moment, the Great, the Immense, the Magnificent. But I immediately came to my senses and I separated one from the other, so smoothly, that with a certain affinity, I left my quick perception behind and I continued experiencing these strange moments.

But the dramatic continuation was an unforgettable first Experience of ascension to a transcendental state for me and remained in my being. And I say the first because in the course of my life, I journeyed through other similar experiences and I followed the same Path, exactly the same Direction and I had the same reactions as everything I described above.

However, I will narrate the continuation of this first experience of mine, of which, as I said, later ones were replicas. Finding myself in this situation, I quickly understood that I was in a region that was familiar, bright, vast and frequented by a strange manifestation of Life, that while it was quite known to me from a long time ago, at that moment, I had no idea how to live it...

Despite the problem I was weighed down with, I felt that I **was living** the **situations** or the **transformations of others** at an **unbelievable speed**, as if I **were flying**, and because of the speed of this endless flight I couldn't determine or sort out what I was feeling. That strange division I felt within me, the feeling that I didn't know how to act and live and, at the same time, that I was living the life of others or of the other world or the very life of the whole Universe, troubled me greatly.

Then I once again heard the familiar **crystalline voice** asking me to listen to it and participate in the **Work** of the **Cause**, of **Creation itself** that at that very moment was forming a **NEW MATRIX of IDEAS** that would constitute the phenomena that **were to be**, in our **physical dimension.**

A **strange emotion overwhelmed** and **shook** me. Then I realized that for the netherworld, I was but a child and that the **power** of **my Being** was limited and imprisoned, not allowed to express itself but, like a camera, it could capture the **Images** of these phenomena that would at some point appear in the physical dimension. Though those were roughly my feelings, I sensed within me a strange strength pushing me and moving not my Being itself, but **MY once forgotten EXPERIENCES.**

A **Sea of Fire** was released from within me then and it undulated with the lights to form very fine and creative **Shapes** and **Designs** and **creations** that for the world of form, our physical world, were unknown and rather useless and foreign. But at that moment, my role was to create these **luminous seas** because they supposedly constituted the creation of **another peculiar Life**.

However, the **Protective Voice** united with me with a **curious joy** and, in the end, I noticed, I realized that I became **ONE** with it and that it was **My very Self**, my **very own Sound**, a voice and a curious rationale or perception that I had, at this very familiar region, which I supposedly frequented from time to time.

Thus, a **Union**, a strange identification, a mutual consciousness of the same perceptions and of the same reactions was formed. It appeared that everything started from me, or rather from this Union, or also from that other, that united or divided me. Like then, I realized that the split of my being was itself a **WHOLE**, a part of which I had become, or we had **absorbed** each other, in the same state, no matter that I was a child and that which was with me was a **BEING**, a **PROTO-FORCE**.

This **joint deed** lasted long and I have full cognizance that during those great moments **I contributed** to the **BIRTH OF THE MATRIX OF IDEAS**. As I described to you, there were two worlds within me as well as two strange and different states that I myself was experiencing then.

The one state was that I had been thrown in a familiar place that I knew and had once lived in. My life then in that place had many similar things to the life of this world, but at a higher vibrational rate and with finer and unrivalled impressions and experiences.

However, the **other** impression–perception, the higher one that stirred me up and penetrated me, dominated and ruled me was that I **was contributing to** something **very General, very Great, very Real** and very **DIVINE.** I felt I had laboured for this creation. But I also felt within me such Admiration for myself.

I was living in the **Kingdom of the Heavens....** .

I can't tell how long this experience lasted. I remember that I passed through the Opening of the Channel of **Fire** under the guidance of the Crystal Voice with **great ease,** in fact, astride the **outer Ray** on which I had ascended during my approach to this region. I arrived in my bedroom and I saw my little body.

I considered **my Being** to be large and I didn't believe that I could fit into such a small vehicle. But I made an effort and I went in. I felt my eyes, my head, my body and my breast tightening so much that I was in pain. Then I began to cry. I didn't have the strength to justify my departure from **THERE,** where, in a way, I was contributing to the very **Creation** of the **Proto-force** of the **GREAT MIND** itself.

Athens, October 21st, 1982
Nikolaos A. Margioris

Note: Nikolaos A. Margioris (1913-1993) was a neo-pythagorean Esoteric Philosopher, an experienced Metaphysical Master and a Christocentric and Christocratic Mystic.

*He established the **neo-pythagorean Philosophical Schools-Omakoios** (from omou – together we hear esoteric-spiritual teachings) of **Athens, Lamia** and **Trikala** where he taught **Esoteric Philosophy** (Esotericism), the **Systems** and the **Practices** of the **Main types** of **Yoga** and **Mysticism** and numerous other **Systems** of **Esoteric Therapeutics** open-handedly, spreading his multifarious knowledge and the wealth of his experiences in the East and in the West, particularly through the filter of his spiritual experiences.*

*His **Omakoios–Schools** continue their operation and the provision of **Esoteric Knowledge** and **Practical Training** without obstruction, while new branches in different parts of Greece have opened up.*

*The body of his written work runs into more than **180 Books** that he wrote within just **23 years** (1970-1993) and whoever is interested can see summaries and the contents of these works in Greek and English on our site: http:// www.omakoio.gr or ask us for a **FREE** copy of the bilingual Greek-English magazine "**New Omakoio**" of 100 pages as a get-to-know-us offer, in which his complete written works and relative articles are included.*

E-mails: omakoio@omakoio.gr *or* omakoeio@gmail.com

DESCRIPTION OF THE EXPERIENCE OF SAMADHI –
THEOSIS OF MASTER NIKOLAOS A. MARGIORIS

(As transcribed in the epilogue
of the second edition of his book
Theurgy Teaches the Eternal Way of the Soul.)

*Transcription – Editing: **Ilias L. Katsiampas***
***Nikolaos A. Margioris'** Student*
*Head of the **Omakoios** of **Trikala** and **Thessaloniki***

Clarification: The Experience that appears below concerns **Nikolaos A. Margioris**, the spiritual Master (1913-
1993), who in his book ***Theurgy Teaches the Eternal
Way of the Soul***, for educational and informative reasons,
describes **his** complete **spiritual Experiences–Samadhi–
Theosis** that he had during his life and which triggered
and were the basis of his prolific written work, fuelling
his tireless desire to teach the **Esoteric Truth** of **Life** and
Creation.

In the present account, N. Margioris' experiences are
described in the **second person**, as if the reader himself
were experiencing them at the same moment, step by step,
so vividly and so excitingly that he feels as if he… is really
and truly participating in the ascension he is observing
and … "experiencing".

Hoping to inform all interested individuals–seekers

of Esotericism, we quote the descriptions exactly as N. Margioris presents them, highlighting the points that we consider of primary importance and deserving of special attention in bold characters or upper case or underlined.

Hermes Trismegistus (thrice-greatest) taught some of his chosen fellow beings real **MYSTICISM**. He gave them **proper instruction** on both **theoretical** and **practical** methods, teaching them how to transcend their conscious state and perceive the **hyperaesthetic vibrations** of the world of form.

Thus, the hypernoetic and hyperaesthetic occult system of **Mysticism**, which the **ancient Greeks** called **THEURGY**, re-emerged. It is the contact man has with **Truth** and **Wisdom** during a particular Mystical or Theurgic deed... .

What does this method of great **Thoth** consist of? It consists of **training** the **Mind**, teaching it to gradually let go of conscious preoccupations and orientate itself to the **hyperconscious**, where the vibrations are finer and immensely quicker than the familiar vibrations of our physical world.

Hyperintellectual activity is **Theurgy** because it provides Divine Works, as its purpose is the accurate perception of the Divine by man. Consciousness helps to a certain extent. However, as soon as the Mind slips beyond its senses, it disappears before the Greatness of the **hypervibrations** that initially appear as **LIGHT**.

Then, the noticeable and the conscious disappear and

an **Unprecedented, Strange Light** with **Infinite Qualities** appears before the altered and dazzled Mind, which it penetrates and permeates with an infinite number of novel stimuli.

Everything becomes LIGHT, but a LIGHT that talks to you, that transfers you, that resolves your questions and your doubts, that completes you and that makes you feel that you have mysteriously healed, that changes you and converts you into just one LIGHT, of which one moment you are a small part of and, at the same time, a huge, infinite and hyper-dimensional LIGHT again.

That is how the **Light** welcomes you, it fills every last bit of **your being** with its **Brightness** and **Knowledge** and **Joy** and **Elation** and **Peace** and **Bliss** and... **Happiness**....

But here the meanings and the known perceptions and impressions must change. And this because a **New Self** appears that in most cases does not look like your other familiar self but that *is* **your very self**. The only difference being that it changed so much that from a worm it became a **Chrysalis**.

Now the **Deep Mystery** is that while you are **Conscious** of the fact that you are who you are, at the same time, you feel deep inside that you are united with your element, which is the real element where you belong, since it has become a **bright LIGHT**, whose dimensions are infinite, and your own dimensions are infinite as well and go where the LIGHT goes.

In this **Infinite LIGHT**, you became Infinite as well and your vastness was so great that it occupied all inexistent space-time and acquainted you with the existent and the inexistent in a matter of seconds, from the moment **Eternity** covered you and fittingly vibrated you, **Blessed** former mortal... .

It is the Work of God... What is God? God is the LIGHT from within which the worlds and the beings emerge, are established and dissolve, appear and fade away, are remade and lost again, within ... inexistent time restrictions and in inconceivable places. Where only **HIS THOUGHTS** have the initiative and the soundless **LOGO-WORD**... They are **His qualities** that behind which, in which, deep within their being have the **Essence**... that is **GOD**...

It is not the flight of your soul into a new world, foreign to the worlds of coarse, or fine, or finer matter. **No.** The **LIGHT** you see, feel, possess, live, use and... **have been converted into** provides you with movement within your immobility and with thoughts within your void of thoughts.

Before you conceive a new thought in your new way of thinking, it gives you the answer that at the same moment is received by you from **countless senses of a new type**, which cannot be compared with the familiar senses of the world of form. Infinite senses of a higher quality – hypersenses – that are filled with LIGHT, which contains stimuli within it, answers that don't need any processes to become perceivable.

This immediately shows that you have become **ONE** with the only **LIGHT** and **ONE** with the only **ONE**, since

thought and **answer** are both **ONE**. As soon as it becomes thought–question–doubt–search, at the same moment it becomes answer–analysis–explanation, so that cause and effect, the inexistent and the existent, God and Deed, spiritsoul and the Mind of God may appear at the same time and simultaneously and identically and inseparably so that you can feel deep inside you that you are everything and everything is you and you are all **ONE**.

You feel something strange, something independent, something unshakeable, something right and true that you just now felt and you live with it. You feel your eternity and **your infinite personality**. Without being divided, without being in any way a separate state, you feel you are something like that, but which, in fact, this something is the **WHOLE One** and you are **ONE** with it, you are **Everywhere**, in the **middle** and at the **edge** and **above** and **below** and **wherever** the **LIGHT** is and... it **Shines** or **Glows** or **Exists**... .

And that's how you started one day or one night from Earth and with a consciousness bound to things of the past on Earth, you reacted and asked for a **hyperconscious** or **hyperintellectual perception** of the **ENTIRE Esodepth**.

Then the other side of your Mind, your hyperconsciousness, your unused hyperintellectual, sprang to life and ran to accept your invitation to... fulfil your new decision. You decided to enter Eternity. The Infinite. Perfection and Truth. To actualize what is beyond the perceivable, the Thence, the Eternal and the Unlimited of space-time and of causality. **Now** you are **LIVING** them and you are swimming without getting wet or tired in the **BEAUTY** and in the **Unrivalled Vastness of Perfection**.

It is the **Work** of God. It is **Theurgy** that carries within it the expressed–manifest **LIGHT** since he himself is LIGHT and from HIS LIGHT everything emerges and again returns and becomes One with HIS LIGHT and HIS LIGHT is "**I AM**".

There are curious states in the whole of LIGHT that derive from the **motionless–moving LIGHT**. While the LIGHT is motionless, it **moves esoterically** with **currents of immense speeds**, which you feel deep within you filling with **Rejuvenating Tremors**. They convey to you all the impressions and stimuli these photo waves find in the **Infinite** and **Vast Systems** and **Spaces** that simultaneously find each other, distance themselves and rediscover each other, all at the same time.

They bring you the innumerable impressions that include familiar situations within them, of very old times, when, at the same time, you had your own reaction–perception, and agreement or disagreement with the tremors that are flooding you even at this moment. Now you accept them pleasantly and you agree with them because they complete what you can now feel, because you became **fit** to **absorb** them on **this ascension of yours**... .

MILLIONS of forms are imprinted within you and each one matches one or more vibrations, or finds itself with them, or is projected by them with its own style, intensity, colour and duration.

These successive forms in the **LIGHT** show you the evolution of the entire human race and remind you of the grades of this evolution that were taught and attended to by our **fellow-being masters.**

At some point, **your own reflections** that you once expressed **also** pass through your mind at lightning speed and you wanted to make sure they were right and true. Now by the alterations in colour tones of all the **LIGHT** that **covers** and **surrounds** you, in a teeny-tiny portion of the LIGHT itself, you see and quickly absorb what their real position is. Sometimes you feel joy, and at other times you feel a negativity about those lost hours of your previous life when you were searching for the truth in **dark** and **barren paths** with your humanmind. At this moment, however, you receive the truth from thousands of directions and within you, it becomes **Sound Knowledge** about everything you had sought and had called difficult problems.

Suddenly, everything changes at the same lightning speed, with the same stability and generality. Your whole being disperses again with great detail in the **Omni flood of light** and you become **ONE** with it. Your assorted thoughts or memories or whatever reactions depart.

Now **YOU ARE Everywhere** and in **Everything.** You know why all these things appear and are shown to you. You are **ONE** with them and it is **your LIGHT** that united with all the **LIGHT** and **you** became **It** and **That** which was initially LIGHT became **you FOREVER.**

And so you united with It. **NOTHING separates you now** and only this Union moves you and takes hold of you. Your wholeness is the truth and it is this truth you know and possess, and this truth vibrates you and is vibrated by you and now you know that **HIS LIGHT** is **YOUR LIGHT** and that **You** and **He** constitute the great **ONE.** Yes, you are now the ONE whose flows–vibrations–tremors make the tremors and the changes in tone of the spirit waves that once surrounded you and now you are both the surrounding and the surrounded....

You have now lost that special position and state that allowed you to see yourself as an observer. Now, observed and observer, you and the whole ONE, you are the only ONE. This is a **living truth** because it is not possible for you to constantly see your own self in your very being.

Now *you* are this whole and the **whole WHOLE** is as you think, but you think of nothing but this **WHOLE,** with which **you** are **ONE.** In this greatness of Unity, you forgot everything, those human relics, and you forgot your trivial preoccupations with the problems that concerned you about the existent and the inexistent.

A **Divine Blessedness,** a **Permanent Peacefulness** now constitutes **your Being.** The **Tremors** are your own **Co-radiations** that make the **LIGHT** alter and simultaneously present tones of infinite colours and reactions to impressions, as many as those born of the tremors you produce and secrete and radiate and diffuse. You are everywhere, the entire length, width, depth, thickness and the whole, only you, you the ONE that united **with It** and constitute the **ONE**....

But this is the crucial moment of the united with the unique **Father–Mother Essence Unit** and **EVERYTHING**. It is the **Supreme Moment** of **Self-confirmation** or the moment of **Proof** that the **Mystic Union** has now become **Permanent** and **Perfect**. At this **Holy Moment**, the one united with the **Father-Mother Essence** feels that he has become a **supreme leader** in **Creation**. And that is what he must automatically **reject** more quickly than the phrase *at once*.

Because if this pleases the individualized united one with the **WHOLE**, if he feels the arrogance and the pride of the worthy, the powerful and the great chosen few who are destined to guide the future, the **Infinite** and the **Eternal** with his until-recently limited being, then his **detachment and his descent immediately** take place and **he is reinstated to the old**, but this is a fall of **failure** and of **inglorious defeat**.

In this **tragic descent**, there is **no benefit** for the poor soul of the **FALLEN ANGEL**. He returned worse off than he was before and he forgot everything and **everything was lost**. The familiar **Darkness** of the individual increased and yesterday's elevated state fell into oblivion and he woke up one morning and was a simple human governed by cold logic, who was not interested in the spiritual kingdoms.

Now, if the spiritsoul is discerned by **its Holy Enthusiasm and if it rejects every selfish initiative** or **interference** in its vibrationally conducted functional Deeds, **THEN** the **UNION** with **Eternity** becomes **unbelievably great** and the **beaming LIGHT Increases Immeasurably and ILLUMINATES...** .

Everything is **Joyful** and **Jubilant** and **Dazzled** with the **Great LIGHT** that pours forth so plentifully from the **spiritsoul** so recently united with the **ONE**–the **WHOLE**.

Everybody and everything Blesses this **Divine Birth** and the **HEAVENS** resound with the **Glory** of this **spiritsoul** that reached the **Crossroads of the Three Hypostases** and showed that it is **CAPABLE of Participating** in the **Great Feast** of the **UNION** and that the division and the avoidance of the ONE ONLY ONE is the disharmony within the **Completed Harmony** of **His Great WORK.**

Great Moments for the **chosen few**, who with **their prudence** and their **true evolution**, entered **deeply** the **Mystery** of **Knowledge** and went through mortality **without dying anymore**, entering the **path** of ETERNITY. There, they will meet the **Essence, Father-Mother**, which has been waiting for them so long....

The restoration of this spiritsoul to the world of form is a **Unique Joy** for **All Humanity**. As soon as the spiritsoul descends into the body that awaits it, the **Mind is enlightened** and SHINES from the **reflection** of the **Radiation** of the substantially and metaphorically enlightened **SPIRITSOUL.**

The humanmind, **as much as it** may conceive, depending on its structure, will be a **Master** among its semi-enlightened brethren and it will preach truths that will be understood with difficult by his fellow beings. **Some** will call him **God** and others will call him **charlatan** and the rest... a fraud.

However, **in essence** we are dealing with a **Superior psycho-spiritual Entity**, which broke the barrier of mortality and crossed over to the other worlds, where **Socrates** and **Plato** talk with **Pythagoras**, their great Master and where **Xenophanes** along with **Parmenides** and **Zeno** of the **Eleatic School** follow them and rejoice with them because even while still on **Earth**, they realized that within the **legendary UNION**, the **Mystery** of the **Divine Revelation** of the **Truth** takes place.

Then there were **antediluvian civilizations** that left to the few who were saved many of their achievements. The **Titans** and others, who bear the symbolic names of antediluvian peoples, had their distinguished ones, who hid their knowledge in the symbols so that they would not be lost by their uninitiated descendants.

Acme and decay of individuals and peoples occurs throughout the course of the millenniums. The incarnated spiritsouls **come** and **go**, proclaiming **HIS** glory ... Let whoever can, follow these **exquisite Sons of God**.

They are Saints, Prophets, Masters, Leaders and God-men. They are His Perfect Children. In order to emulate them, we must enter the realm of **Mysticism–Meditation** so as to avoid the embrace of matter and free ourselves from its eternal slavery.

Onwards we go, let us not waste time. **Let us** all **reject** the world of falsehood and deceit, the world of hypocrisy and malevolent egoism.

Let us embrace Humility and **Sacrifice** and let us use the **invaluable LOVE**. Then we shall enter the vibrations of **HIS Heart** and we shall become **real brothers of Jesus Christ...** .

Nikolaos A. Margioris
May 1987

DESCRIPTION OF THE SPIRITUAL EXPERIENCE
OF MASTER NIKOLAOS A. MARGIORIS

(As transcribed in the chapter
"*The Necessity of Mysticism*" of the second
edition of his book *Theurgy Teaches the
Eternal Way of the Soul*.)

Transcription – Editing: Ilias L. Katsiampas
Nikolaos A. Margioris' Student
Head of the Omakoios of Trikala and Thessaloniki

Clarification: The Experience that appears below
concerns Nikolaos A. Margioris, the spiritual Master
(1913-1993), who in his book **Theurgy Teaches the
Eternal Way of the Soul**, for educational and informative reasons, describes his complete spiritual Experiences–Samadhi–Theosis that he had during his life
and which triggered and were the basis of his prolific
written work and fuelled his tireless desire to teach the
Esoteric Truth of **Life** and **Creation.**

Hoping to inform all interested individuals–seekers
of Esotericism, we quote the descriptions exactly as N.
Margioris presents them, highlighting the points that
we consider of primary importance and deserving of
special attention in bold characters or upper case or
underlined.

DESCRIPTION OF THE SPIRITUAL EXPERIENCE OF MASTER NIKOLAOS A. MARGIORIS

The soul patiently waits for the **Mind** to make a **turn-around** toward the BEYOND in order to offer it vibrations of **amazing Peace** and **Happiness.**

When this happens at some moment, our world changes and the split between matter and the spirit is lost. Then a **NEW sensation,** which doesn't match those we know and does not come from earthly reactions, appears before us. It **is** an **Otherworldly Vibrational Perception** that brings **Messages** from the other World, and as a result, the mortal of yesterday becomes worthy of the **Hyperessence and the Eternal.**

In this **New Christening** of **human existence** in the **Divine Baptistery,** which contains the **Clear Spirit** instead of water, man feels himself **converting** and **dematerializing with unbelievable speed** and with unparalleled force, which gives him the sensation that he has experienced an incredible change–revival. He broke the barriers of matter and mortality and in an inexistent time period, he entered the **Beyond** and **Heaven** and he ascertained that **Eternity** with its **Truth** is identical to the unbelievable **PERFECTION.** This is the role of **Mystical Actualization,** this is the Necessity of Mysticism.

The doors of death **closed** and those of **immortality opened.** The joyful spiritsoul sends a multitude of waves that entrance and amaze the **dazzled Mind**. **Illumination** upon **illumination** and **Enlightenment** upon **Enlightenment** enter ceaselessly the newly transformed area of the Mind, and fill **all** its **Archives** with what we in our human language call **Wisdom**.

Man suddenly ascended to the heights of other vibrations, whose content is different to what he knew until then. Everything shows us that beyond the known frontiers of our world, there is a state of greater perfection, whose vibrations are much higher than ours and contain the **Light** of **Knowledge** that leads to **Truth** within them.

You remain stunned and dumbfounded and wonder-struck before the **new Enlightenment** that offers **KNOWLEDGE** that cannot be uttered and that carries the distinctions of **legendary Wisdom**. Your Mind of yesterday **ceases** to guide you with sensory impressions and your old thoughts **no longer** produce the limited knowledge of the world of form that you lived in until recently....

The **caterpillar** became a **chrysalis**, but in the **Spiritual meaning** now of the conversion. **You fully experience** the **Mysteries** of **your Mystical Life** and you are **connected** with **thousands of Minds of supreme worth**, which **all** form the **WHOLE** and the **ONE**.

Little by little, you enter **Truth** and, before your eyes, **Perfection** becomes **Immense** and only **ONE**. You forgot that you were a human being, that you had a name, that you lived with a body and with rich knowledge about the world and its boundaries.

Now you feel that you entered **another World**, that your thinking lost its enquiring system, and changed, and became **Otherworldly** and **Universal** and **Exouniversal** and **Omnicreative** and... it has **no** relation now to your old self.

You **feel** the **Infinite** and the **Eternal as if it were you** and the **pulses** of **Omnicreation** are **your own pulses** and you live in an entire **Omnithought** in an **Omnimind** that **has** supplied you with all those **powers of His**, which you could never have imagined even a little time ago.

Little by little, you feel that you grew up so much, that you are within the whole of creation and now quickly, very quickly, instead of feeling, you see the **Unsaid** and the **Hidden**. Worlds appear with infinite beings like a **LIGHT**, where everything is **self-luminous** and... passes through your being and goes by uninterruptedly, sometimes they go and sometimes they come, as if to ask for your opinion and your guidance.

However, all these things **unite with you** and you know that they constitute your very being, which is that of those who unceasingly move their own being. Thus, soon, everything becomes **ONE**, both what comes and what goes and they reinforce your absolute certainty that everything constitutes you.

In this Mystical State, you are Serene, Calm and Blissful since you know that all these things that are occurring are **MOST NATURAL** and that they are in your being and you find yourself, at the same time, in your own being. You know all these things and they know you and they are not unfamiliar to you anymore. You know that you are all you contain and all that contains you.

This is your Mystical Awakening. It brought your real existence to your being and now you perceive that the speed of the infinite conversions that take place before you cannot be secured in your physical Mind that has been overwhelmed with absolute ecstasy, and can only see, feel, notice a new sensation that has suddenly emerged, but it doesn't know how to react to this **unimaginable presentation** that occurs inside and out, above and below, ahead and behind, high and low, near and far, and everywhere where there is no emptiness, and nothing foreign and distant and unknown.

No initiative, doubt, objection, disagreement, reaction **exists** since **EVERYTHING** is **Right, Fair, Perfect, Beautiful, Ideal, containing** everything and, at the same time, **contained** in **EVERYTHING**. With **LIGHT** and only LIGHT, a LIGHT that does not blind but that fills and speaks and contains many Worlds, Universes and Dimensions, within which **HIS LIGHT** exists, that which is the **LIGHT of everything**, yet **YOUR LIGHT**, which fills you with **Strength, Light** and **Wisdom**, and that does not illuminate you because you are the **Hearth** from which everything emanates and ... derives.

You don't swim in the LIGHT because you are the LIGHT and everything that leaves or comes to you constitutes your being and everything is united, even your voice itself, which is the voice of all the worlds and of the beings, as are your thoughts.

At the end and in the innermost parts, you are one with your near and distant pulse. You receive pulses and vibrations and you create pulses and vibrations, just like everything around you pulsates and changes. Worlds and Worlds and Creations and Changes and Replacements and Eternal Activity that fills you with thousands of unknown sensations that you now feel working uninterruptedly, filling you with information of another kind, which contains within it **Infinite Features**, like speech, lights, shapes and changes that, without being specific forms, **remind you** or **awaken within you** or are **revived within you** and **represent** things that you knew but were locked up somewhere and now they sprang to life **in perfection** near you to all become **ONE** with you, with **Love**, with much Love, yes, only **ONE**.

Then, you also feel a **VOICE** that is similar to the one you once knew as yours, which ceaselessly seems to explain and to remind you of strange old contacts and moments of yours, when you were **ONE** with the **WHOLE** and in that ONE, you played the role of the participant and partner and the absolute conjoint of **His Self**.

Without seeing you see, and **without** hearing you

hear, and **without** going **you are** EVERYWHERE and you **give directions** and you take advice and again you hear and rehear your own voice fading away in the distance... .

...Come take your place and look at the **Worlds** and the **Beings** that congregate inside and work for your eternal purpose. **Stand with them** and **help them remember** their **initial Greatness** and to **return** to their **great Reality**, where in the WHOLE ONE they will meet their **Eternal Beginning–Principle**. This will be their respite until their new revivification begins, when, with you, they will descend to bring the news to the **Eternal HEARTH** that will be awaiting the news again. The cycle is composed of neither decay nor incorruptibility. It is One and always the same throughout its entire unique undulation.

Is there some way for the mystical experiences of our spiritsoul to be conveyed to our physical world. The answer is **NO**. No Mind and language and letters and meanings can present and explain the **multidimensional events** that take place in the systems **Beyond Omnicreation**. Those events are different from these events.

The Mind can grasp only a small part and present it with its usual interpretation, thoughts and language. But what is formulated is an approximation; it is somewhat **RELEVANT**. It does not contain a multidimensional hypostasis and it doesn't bring things to Mind like its subconscious does.

Should I call the information that these countless vibrations convey to the Mind **psycho-sensations?** The curious and full and – in many aspects – mature, multidimensional information that carries Light, Sound, Qualities, Explanations, Consubstantial representative descriptions, Images with countless colours and thousands of other complementary, rich stimuli that enter your spiritsoul and intoxicate and move the Mind that tries, in vain, to render it in a certain language.

..."It was the **twenty-fourth** of **March in 1967, Saturday**, at **eleven** at **night**. I was reading the research from the **manuscripts** or the **papyri** that had been found in **Qumran**, in the Dead Sea, near and on the heights that protected the camp of the **Esseans** from the winds in the times of... **Jesus Christ.**

...At about **two o'clock**, I began to **meditate** and at some point during my meditation, I felt myself **drifting away** and **leaving** my conscious state. I had closed my eyes long before. I was sitting on the carpet and I was leaning against the bed. The little light of the icons from the iconostasis was shimmering and not one clock distracted me. Faraway noises were heard from time to time until even they died down and a sense of peacefulness reigned within me. Then **everything was forgotten** and **the walls of the house opened.** Outside the now inexistent house, there was only **LIGHT** unlike any other we know. A **LIGHT** that contained **EVERYTHING** within it. It passed through me and gave me **not** only information about where I was and how I was, but also **incredible Powers, Knowledge** and **Stimuli** that came from EVERYWHERE, from the only ONE and the WHOLE, which I had EN-TERED unwittingly.

Then I felt within me that I **was growing** and unit-ing with the **Immense Spaces**, which I couldn't see though I lived within them, knew them and followed their incessant and extremely rapid **leaps.**

That **LIGHT**, the **Uncreated** and the **Eternal LIGHT**, was speaking and creating, was changing and dissolving **EVERYTHING** with incredible speed and great Experi-ence, as if it knew what it was doing so well, as if it were the movement of its hand or of its foot.

The worlds that it was recreating, after it had dis-solved them a little time ago, and the beings that it was forming in Cyclical Rhythms were so quick and so Per-fect and so vivid and so true that they were proof that they were products of their true maker, this incredible **LIGHT**. I was within it and within it I existed. I was a part of it and I stopped believing that I was something separate, something partial that had just arrived. I be-lieved that I had always been like that and I knew so well what was going on now that even before they took place, I knew with certainty how they would appear with the great One **LIGHT**, in which I had **expanded** and I was filling all its being, and I felt it was all in my being and that it was all being filled with my own being. I had united, having a vague sense of that some-thing I was supposed to be.

I **saw** with the **eyes** of the **soul** the **CAUSES** that make the phenomena of this world. Everything we know is the result. That is where we find the Causes, the Different vibrations that prepare the Causes like Wave manifestations, the Originals that will become the morphic shapes, the results in our world.

A **perpetual rhythm-motion** that carries Everything within it vibrates Eternally from the **LIGHT** of **Omnicreation** that has the **Knowledge**, the **Wisdom**, the **Perfection** as well as the **Justice** it uses when it performs **Its Work** within it.

This obscure perception, this strange actualization, this Necessity of Mysticism brings the individual man in touch with the **TOTALITY**, the now uniform coexistence of the observer and the observed.

Everywhere Everything is **ONE**. The observer is the same **ONE** as the observed. He has the impression that he conveys what he wants, but that is exactly the will of the ONE and thus there is nothing else than this alone since the separate parts find themselves united in the dominion of the **WHOLE ONE**.

That is exactly what the **Mystical Union** of the being of man with the Absolute and the Vast **SUBSTANCE** is. It is from this perception of the union of the Creator with the creature that all Knowledge of Truth derives. That's why it is called the **NECESSITY OF MYSTICISM.**

Only this Union teaches and permeates and enlightens and perfects and elevates and immaterializes and illuminates and liberates the creature from the vanity of the world of hylomorphism.

With **true introspection**, with our well-known **KNOW YOURSELF**, with our **purification** of sly and materialistic thoughts and with **words of a spiritual** content and **wise meanings** and with **actions of perfection**, man will **become worthy** of **attaining** his **Mystical Union**.

His Mystical elevation is a necessity because only in this way will man find the true **LIGHT** of **Knowledge**. When he arrives, at some point, after proper preparation, to the **Divine Chambers**, where the **Spirit** is completely separated from the low vibrations of matter, then everything will be different. Everything changes and the small human life turns into an **ETERNAL** one since it will forever be included in **Eternity**.

Ignorance and deprivation of the truth give man the impression of mortality. However, behind and above it, there is the **Everlasting Truth** that every mortal is truly mortal in external appearance. His other, his true hypostasis is Immortal, Eternal and Unshakeable. That is the **Primary Truth**.

But is that all? Everything around us is an apparent state, perishable and renewed. But in reality, there is an **Unshakeable SUBSTANCE**, on which the supposed solid goods of human life are based, change, deteriorate and regenerate.

Everything changes, and regenerates, and slips away, and is replaced, and replicas appear, while deep down everything is foreign to what existed a little while back. It is the cycle all of us go through and fulfil. When we are born and when we die. When we are strengthened and when we are enfeebled. When we come and when we go. However, deep inside, all of us know that our transience is a certainty. This has become consciousness for us and it gives us the secret hope of a more real life waiting for us somewhere there.

As soon as our fellow being is able to learn the Truth, he immediately mutates and becomes something else. He turns inwards and struggles to find the **Secret Outlet**, the path toward **Liberation**, and that's when he recognizes the ... Necessity of Mysticism....

Yes, this is what helps man to escape the heartache of doubt, to feel that he is participating in **Eternity** and that his present life is the blurry shadow of His **Eternal Being**.

It was the Necessity of Mysticism that led him to the heights of truth and that revealed the place of his origin. He actualized what he once did not believe and did not realize. Now, with the ascension to spirituality, now that he is certain that life and its phenomena are an allegoric manifestation of an integral reality, now that he knows that the **Beyond** he read about is the **Only Truth**. The current and the tangible and the temporary, the momentary and the transient are morphic presentations and, apart from their continual external mutations, are in essence, **pseudo-shields** of a reality, whose purpose it is to represent its dreams with soluble smoke.

As you noticed, I showed you how the inside works and what the outside looks like. There is an analogy between the below and the above. Between the visible and the invisible. They have proportions and they form the **analogical philosophy** of **Ammonius Saccas**. The legendary **Hermes Trismegistus** or **Thoth** said in **His Smaragdine Table**:

"That which is below is like that which is above ..."

My dear reader, you can introspect your inner Self and reveal it. Then you will realize that your outer mummy is a temporary cover of **Your Inner Immortal Greatness**. But as soon as you recognize your true Self, then you enter Eternity and you leave transiency.

With this **magnificent volte-face**, man changes from weak and becomes strong and from mortal he becomes immortal. He has full responsibility, it is the right and the garland of glory that he will receive, it rightly belongs to him. Behind this temporariness, eternity exists. I narrated it to you in the first part of this Mystical chapter that I named the NECESSITY OF MYSTICISM in order that you perceive it.

BY THE SPIRITUAL MASTER N. A. MARGIORIS:
DESCRIPTION OF THE FIRST EXPERIENCE
OF THE AWAKENING OF MAN'S PSYCHIC VISION

(As published in the chapter "In Esotericism they
are contained and from its essence are derived
the Terrestrial, the Extra-terrestrial and mainly
the Hyper-terrestrial" of the second edition of
Nikolaos A. Margioris' book *The Other View of
Erich Von Daniken's Dogma*.)

*Transcription – Editing: **Ilias L. Katsiampas**
Nikolaos A. Margioris' Student
Head of the **Omakoios** of **Trikala** and **Thessaloniki***

Clarification: The Experience that appears below is derived from the experiential perception of **Nikolaos A.
Margioris**, the spiritual Master **(1913-1933)**, who, for
educational and informative reasons, in his book *The
Other View of Erich Von Dainiken's Dogma*, describes
all his **spiritual Openings–Experiences** that concern
the **first true awakening** of the **psychic vision** of any
person who is interested in perceiving and familiar-
izing oneself with the **Esoteric Truth** of **Life** and the
Mysteries of **Creation**.

It is a **unique** and **rare opportunity** for any interested individual or researcher of Esotericism to observe

and become informed through the step-by-step account and the relevant analytical description as N. Margioris himself presents it.

We highlight the points that we consider of primary importance and deserving of special attention in bold characters or in uppercase or by underlining.

DESCRIPTION OF THE AWAKENING
OF MAN'S PSYCHIC VISION

On the **first awakening** of **our psychic vision**, we immediately see and we immediately meet **in the very world** we live in **now** the **first invisible phenomena** that a little while before, in our natural wakefulness, we didn't even dare to imagine.

For many years, scientists have studied and experimented with the well-known aura of the physical being, without ever learning about it, despite the bizarre physical machines they invented.

However, the first person that will be awakened will **immediately** observe that every individual emits a **luminous multicoloured aureole** that looks like a **lace of fire** or as if it radiates a **continuous array of spear-like leaves** of a **fiery brightness** that are sometimes extended and sometimes shortened, depending on the **health** and the **thoughts** of our fellow being. For a moment, the most vivid are separated, those that prevailed moments before, and they look somehow wilted, a sign of some abnormality, irritation or repentance, and everything changed.

Instead of the continuous multifarious colouration we saw in the aura, some coloured currents suddenly appear, first in a bright red colour, then a little brighter and finally it changes into a thousand variations till it disappears, bringing new photo-coloured effusions, mixed and lively, until it becomes a uniform sky blue colour that turns into deep blue and fades into a deep dark grey.

But now, again suddenly, new waterfalls of other colourations begin to flow, changing according to the feelings that are continually reproduced and alternate in man, with thoughts he ceaselessly produces with every passing moment.

Soon, he who is having the psychic vision sees that **thousands of beings**, strange and multicoloured, vibrating according to the colour they belong to, hover around every individual. The **products** of our **thoughts** and **imagination** are like an indivisible tight, fluid, vibrating and multicoloured chain, a **creation** of our **desire** and **passion**.

They are **disgusting monsters**, products of hate and black evil, and other vengeful polymorphous, forked-tongued aberrations that have terrifying expressions, strange figures, somehow better than the previous ones, with nicer faces, more able-bodied and more human, that quickly cede their place to other harmonious and more beautiful figures, with perfect colourations, at times blue, at times white, at times yellow and finally they become golden and finally end up a milky colour that shines like the night stars.

Still, he who has the psychic vision sees that the individual's aura seems to be targeted by and the destination of **other** similar **multicoloured images** that look exactly like those that at that very moment whirl around the face and the head of the individual, while others remain permanently near the individual himself, as if forever united with him, and others, strangely enough, leave immediately, with immeasurable speed, as if they don't match.

All these incessant shimmers that are sowed around us by us ourselves, in this great expanse and in a different state, constitute the intensity of various thoughts of all types, of our psychosynthesis, continually sowed and pulsating with their own rhythm, the one we gave them during their birth.

Thus, **without** realizing it, **we beget worlds, good**, **bad**, mediocre or naive, which we sometimes join and obey.

If only **Esotericism** could show you your **great mistake** from here! **Don't** think evil. **Don't** send forth new armies of evil. **Don't** sow hatred. **Give LOVE** in order to bring the **Paradisiac Epoch** on **Earth**.

Many people call this psychic vision, this unknown sensor that not only sees through matter but sees beyond the Universe to other Dimensions of the Esodepth, the Third Eye, the Projection of Consciousness, Psychic vision, Clairvoyance, Esoconsciousness, Subconsciousness, etc.

If the **neophyte**, who awakens his **clairvoyant ability** for the first time, casts a **psycho-glance** at another man, he will see his Internal bodily organs pulsating and he will know which of them are ailing or even useless. He will also see that around the individual's body there are other strange flame wrappings that are separated and move in their own pulsing and vibrating way and they communicate with each other with fiery marks as if they were umbilical cords and as if one is always feeding the other with their strange colourful fire and the light they hold within them.

A **new world** appears before us. To those lacking psychic vision or clairvoyant ability, it is utterly foreign. Countless odd, disgusting and black **beings**, polymorphous with black limbs, pass before us at lightning speed, trying to adhere to somebody in order to save themselves and not dissolve in the fiery astral currents that dissolve these inconceivable monsters on their passage.

As soon as the psychic vision is satisfied with this first vision it has, it becomes restless, wanting to see more of the peculiar happenings surrounding it, which were unknown and inexistent just a little while before.

The soul goes through the impenetrable constructions, a spiritual ray, and it meets the ailing bedridden one, and at that moment, he takes his last breath on his deathbed (he is dying). At the same moment, it is surprised to see, for the first time, that life and the soul leave in a different manner than the one he knew until then.

A multicoloured electromagnetic force is separated from the atoms and the cells of a person and is concentrated in **three parts** of his **physical body**.

One of these three **parts** is the **head**. The **second point** is the **chest**, probably on the left, and the **third point** of concentration is the abdomen, where they talk to us about a solar plexus, a characteristic part of man.

In little physical time, these **three luminous points** appear to see each other and each one tries to bring the others toward it so that relatively soon, the three luminous points converge and form **a triangle** of **coloured light**, with the **peak** on the **chest** or on the **plexus** or on the **head**.

If the peak of this triangle forms on the head, the colour that prevails is **white**. If it forms on the chest, the colour will be **dark blue**. If it forms on the plexus, **red**.

In a few seconds of place-time, this **photo-triangle** emerges from the point where its peak formed, where it gets its colouring from. This light emerges from the physical body with a **distinct spasm** and immediately takes refuge in the first multicoloured luminous net-like wrapping, through which it passes, taking another form and from a triangle it becomes completely round, keeping the colour it had as it was leaving the physical body, a luminous triangle.

Nearly at the same moment, a **slow, drawn-out sigh** and a **characteristic humming** are heard, as if something has broken, and that's when the **coloured ball** rapidly leaves the **netlike multicoloured hypostasis** and enters another casing of **fire** and **light** that looks like the light when the stars appear.

All this took place at as much speed as the observer needed to observe that the passage of life–the soul itself took place in these tubes–umbilical cords that connect the casings, the luminous bodies that surround our physical body.

Now, the **second umbilical cord** was also cut, the one that connected the netlike casing with the second starlit one in which the **small luminous ball** seems to shine especially bright.

At the same moment, the physical body remained **lifeless** and **deadened** since all its life was absorbed from the netlike body and then from the strange astral body.

Now the separation takes place near the ground. The astral body leaves in a flash, leaving the corpse lying like a relic on Earth, with its replica of the phosphorescent ethereal net hovering over it like a roof, but slowly beginning to lose its intensity and little by little disappearing with luminous explosions.

Within the bodies of the remaining luminous fiery astral bodies that received it and of the remaining others that we shall describe another time, we can easily distinguish a **resplendent white-coloured point (dot),** which is the **immortal soul**, now very distant from physical life.

One phenomenon has ended. **Death has been executed** with all its luminous confirmations and the summoning and the transition of the human soul from its physical casing to the luminous netlike ethereal one, and from this one, within seconds of earthly time, it took cover in the astral casing and settled there permanently, cutting off every contact with the two external and more lowly bodies: the netlike–ethereal one and the physical–dead one.

Now the spiritsoul entered its new astral body, the fourth dimension, where it forgot its three-dimensional stroll and it began its new birth in its astral world.

But as soon as this spectacle ended, the psychic vision, having observed everything up until the departure of a sister spiritsoul for the astral dimension and the mechanism of how it occurred, abruptly fell to physical life and involuntarily entered a **new perambulation** of this same world, not in today's contemporary time, but in **very ancient times, millions of years** ago, when other beings and creatures of the physical kingdoms were on Earth.

Psychic vision or Clairvoyance, the Third Eye or the New sense, the Sixth sense now gives us images from a very ancient epoch of our Earth, with the kingdoms that constitute it – **mineral, vegetative, animal** – in great activity.

The forests are countless, they almost cover the

Earth and every tree is close, very close to the other, as if wishing to be embraced. They are very tall, almost fifty metres in height, and a deep green colour with very dense foliage.

In this physical dominion, everything works to produce chlorophyll, and the atmosphere is full of its scent and all of life is enclosed within the plant Kingdom.

Redemption from the physical enslavement of the **vegetative life** of the **green kingdom** takes place with **thunder** as the saviour and the initial application with **lightning**.

Thus, an **endless fire** begins to liberate all captive life from the forest, burning this hard kingdom with spite and releasing all captive life.

Soon, **incessant rain** puts a stop to the exterminator and hands over the dominant life to the creator, restoring power to life in the entire surrounding area.

The terrible **Enceladus** begins to growl and suddenly the ground yields and Mother Earth takes immense expanses of the forests in the area into its bowels, while in their initial place, fires appeared from the depths of the Earth, then **lava**, multicoloured and unbridled, vehement and violent, with immeasurable smoke and dust, fiery dust.

Thus, the same ever-creative life suddenly allows the indispensable annihilator to take the initiative and bring change, and to release whatever was bound on Earth.

With another psycho-glance at the **same epoch**,

another life activity is observed, the **nourishment** of the **big trees**. The great activity in the roots of every type of vegetation and the conversion of so-called dead matter into living matter and of its transfer to the tall trunks, to the branches and to the foliage constitutes a new revelation of the presence and the direction of everything by the **FIRST MIND**.

The incessant flow of the surrounding minerals and fluids to the roots of every plant triggers admiration and wonder. It's as if the minerals and the fluids are obliged to approach and to enter the subterranean factories of the trees, where at hydroelectric speed they change directly into colour and heat and other combinations and they are sent with immense pressure to the neurons of vegetative organisms.

This perpetual process of the ascension and distribution of all kinds of prepared nourishment from the roots, as I said before, to the foliage presupposes a **dynamic life** of this food-supplied tree, which is easily ascertained by psychic vision now that it sees the mystery that takes place in the foliage with the production of chlorophyll.

How the juices ascend to such heights, to find the branches and the foliage, to be absorbed, and to change into wood, is a real mystery of nature, which the human intellect can now see before it because it has psychic vision as a tool.

This proves the real hypostasis of the tree, whose instinct correctly and judiciously provides it with a truly wise energy that develops the tree, supplies it with nutrition and keeps it alive.

The patient and fearless seeker of clairvoyance or psychic vision sees right before him the **orgasm** of **life** itself continuing without interruption everywhere.

From these juices and mixtures in the roots of every tree, from the waste and faeces and the other elements taken from the mineral and the fluid elements, new branches and twigs suddenly shot out of the tree, new foliage sprouted and new casings surrounded its trunk in order to protect it.

The noise that takes place when matter is being metabolized and the foods-juices ascend, when they quickly convert into limbs and leaves, when chlorophyll is produced, is deafening and is heard incessantly with great intensity and rhythm all around, covering everything. This is the renowned ability called **CLAIRAUDIENCE** or our well-known **PSYCHIC HEARING**.

I wonder if it is only these things that our physical fellow being doesn't see, doesn't hear and doesn't feel. Or perhaps other things take place all around us that were man aware of them, he would quickly change his actions, taking other paths than those that he has chosen to follow so persistently.

Is it possible, perhaps, that we aren't, as we believe, alone and beside us **thousands** of **beings** come and go and walk around, psychic bodies of course, but with intellect and above all wisdom, that when they see our deeds, feel sorry for us and wait for us to be enlightened, to become superior and somewhat wiser?

But even here in front of us in the physical life, the clairvoyant sees them and is surprised. Below the surface of the physical ground, another cosmogony of our natural world is taking place. A few centimetres below the surface, thousands of beings take nutrients from the plant roots; they take the waste, the decaying foliage, the useless fruit and all the excrements of the tree and they multiply and they live within their own world, in families and genera and races and when they die, they give their body back to the tree from which they took everything and subsisted. This gratitude to the food source, the tree, must move every spiritual soul.

Thus, psychic vision observes the great cycle, the recycling, in all life forms. Everything that evaporated, again became water–life after a short time; it returned to the same elements from which it had been separated and reunited with what we call matter.

The same cycle always, permanently and continually, is repeated under the same physical laws that always execute the **eternal work** of the **Divine Mind** with prudence and careful thought.

In other words, as physical people, we are cognizant of and can conceive almost none of the phenomena around us.

Of course, we can't achieve this because, as I have very often stated in my written work, not all of us, most fellow beings, possess **hypersenses**; that is, doors and windows in our physical psychic Being, through which other information may enter and make us aware of the endless events of our own physical world taking place around us.

This continual process of the multiplicity of the worlds is the uninterrupted multicreation of the world of form, whose purpose it is to maintain the formed manifestation of **BREATH** itself.

Perhaps we all possessed knowledge of these occurrences taking place around us in past times, when this clairvoyant hypersense **functioned** in all our fellow beings.

Today, for unknown and forgotten reasons, the inner senses don't operate save in a few individuals and in rare cases.

Thus, with this disadvantage and the heavy loss of these means, we don't have the knowledge that we need.

It is not possible for us to extend these hypersenses to the **Galactic systems** of the entire formed world and to know of the existence and the activity of all beings.

Today, we cannot even extend our individual consciousness to the ends of our planet Earth, of **our Galaxies** and to all parts of the entire **formed Universe**, to the plethora of systems of the **Esodepth**, to the eso-dimensions, as I present them in my writing, where other different worlds from our own Earthly world exist.

We lack all these and many other things that are

much more serious and somewhat exciting if they become known by our own Earthly world.

Note: Nikolaos A. **Margioris** *(1913-1993) was a neo-pythagorean Esoteric Philosopher, an experienced Metaphysical Master and a Christocentric and Christocratic Mystic.*

*He established the neo-pythagorean **Philosophical Schools–Omakoios** (from omou-together we hear the esoteric-spiritual teachings) of **Athens**, **Lamia** and **Trikala** where he taught **Esoteric Philosophy** (Esotericism), the **Systems** and the **Practices** of the Main Types of **Yoga** and **Mysticism** and numerous **Systems** of **Esoteric Therapeutics**, open-handedly sharing his multifarious knowledge and the wealth of his experiences in the East and in the West, particularly through the filter of his spiritual experiences.*

*His **Omakoios–Schools** diligently continue their operation and the provision of **Esoteric Knowledge** and **Practical Training**, while new branches have been opened up in different parts of Greece.*

*The body of his written work totals more than **180 Books** that he wrote within just **23 years** (1970-1993) and whoever is interested can see summaries and contents in Greek and in English on our site: http://www.omakoio.gr or ask us to send him a **FREE** copy of the bilingual Greek-English magazine "**New Omakoio**" of 100 pages as an introductory* *gift, in which the total of his written work and related articles are included.*

E-mails: omakoio@omakoio.gr *or* omakoeio@gmail.com

BOOK MYSTICAL TEACHINGS–VOLUME A
"PERCEPTION OF PERMANENCE"

I am writing on December 9th 1987, in the parlour of my home. It is half past three in the morning. Sitting across from me is my daughter Kallia, who, while keeping me company during my illness, is painting an icon of Saint Nikolaos.

For a long time now, I have been meditating on the existence of the world and the beings that constitute the world and the separate infinite points that form all these worlds.

What is the relationship between the worlds and the beings? What connects them and what separates them? Where is the Centre and where is the remote region? Do they have the same vibrations and the same concentration in strength and effectiveness or are they islets that remain independent and separated from their origin?

That's how my meditation carries me away and into thoughts that escape the enclosed confines of logic and they push me to leap outward, where everything is foreign to this logic and where an alien world is waiting to again take me with it tonight... to the amazing Mystery of Transcendental Life.

I meditate deep, continuously, without interruption and I try to enter the vortex of the life of Forms, not like I feel it as a man, from my point of view, but as a conditional part of the whole world that I am just at this very moment starting to... experience.

Now my meditation is ascending, as am I with it, and I reach the point where I can again see this SOMETHING that I was living just recently, this quick moment of my inexistent hypostasis.

My thoughts are much stranger than they were last night. Now, a moment ago, I am beginning to learn how to connect with the deep mystery of existence. What exactly is being transformed within me every passing second?

A new man springs forth and a new world then appears. Two worlds, different from the old, two foreign places and other places that are essentially similar and so familiar that they know where they come from and where they are going. The old self observes and agrees. It knows that the world that is emerging is his deeper and truer self that has been absent for such a long time.

Now, on my initial ascent, new, curious impressions overwhelm me. Really... Did you ever contemplate, as I am doing now, thinking deeply and realizing... that nothing exists without it being existent? But what does it mean that something exists and is existent? Meanings and ideas and thoughts and presentations and form confirmations and amorphous existences and morphic presentations, they are all the same and they don't differ from each other, save in the corresponding perception of PERMANENCE.

Everything belongs to an unchangeable situation where everything falsely changes momentarily and this change follows a rule and a series of well-ordered changes that in their unfolding will cover their existence, forming their entire evolutionary course, which is infinite, in order to come back to its initial departure, which is imposed.

That is the perception of permanence. Everything that is conceived, known and unknown, new and old, existent and inexistent, nothing else but the unfolding and folding in their eternity and in their self-substance and their inexistent hypostasis that is the only consistent hyperreality.

According to the area of Omnicreation, whatever is expressed is inexistent and doesn't exist and only what is not expressed exists. As you may realize, all the things we perceive don't exist and what we don't perceive are the only things that exist.

Everything becomes perceivable by the state of our Mind and, in fact, by its proper functioning. The small and simple vibrations and perception of these vibrations are suitable for extroverted and unevolved Minds. Therefore, the conceived morphic shapes by the extroverted Minds are of insignificant vibrations, of the lowest and the most primitive morphic presentations.

The more elevated the Mind is, the more perfection does the conception of the vibrations bring. Perfect morphic images that touch the edges of the Blueprints, of the correct platonic ideas, the stirrings produced by perfection.

I bring something that is happening to your attention. But what is happening is suitable for and suited to your perception. It is your identification with or your simulated vibration to the wavelength of some produced vibration.

These vibrations are an infinitesimal part of the whole of Vibrations that take place in the infinite area of their occurrence. Only a tiny part of their occurrence is perceived by us in order to warn us about the occurrence of permanence.

An infinitesimal crack in an inexistent suitable moment brings the connection of the Mind–Soul–Eternity–Substance–Spirit and Permanence. This Holy Moment mutually vibrates the part with the WHOLE, the inner basis of the part with the whole existing ONE.

Mysticism is this moment, this crack, it is this mutually vibrating emotion, it is the reception and the conveyance of Knowledge and perception, from the permanent to the temporary, from the deceptive to the Real, from the Eternal to the temporary, from the existing to the inexistent and from the real to the artificial, from the invariable to the variable.

BOOK MYSTICAL TEACHING–VOLUME A
"COSMIC GOOD AND EVIL"

On December 17th 1974, which is exactly twelve years ago because today is the 17th of December 1986, a gentleman who had formed an interesting movement around him at that time came into my office. He asked me what I was exactly and how I judged the world. He asked me to write it down on a paper for him at that very moment, which I did immediately, since that was what his soul so desired. He was the unforgettable **Mr Adamandios Karamourtzounis.** This is what I wrote as my written reply, as he so desired:

"**17/12/1974:** From a very young age, I have been following the only true path toward perfection, the difficult path of **God.**

Within me, I very often hear **His Voice,** which sometimes approves and sometimes rejects my intentions. So, in every difficult moment of my decisions, I turn to **HIM,** the only **Knower** of the **correct** and **true side** of **Everything.**

He truly lives within me, it is **HE** who with a **Ray of His Eternal Light** guides my steps and **directs my thoughts** and **my deeds, my words.** What is happening to me? My faith is great and unceasing and I fully accept whatever happens to me in life. Perhaps with this belief I have, I am guided surely toward the good road.

With this faith I have, I can... Be healed if I am taken ill. Achieve miracles, always for the good of my fellow beings, when I ask to do so, of my Lord and my God, of my Beloved Master, **Jesus Christ.**

With His assistance and His grace, I can become rejuvenated, become a new man in body but particularly in Mind. Thus, I will be able to help thousands of my fellow beings recover from illness, addiction and other passions, and I may have the pleasure of witnessing their return to Christ."

The perfection and the harmony that is found in experience and knowledge is acquired slowly, just as the greatest enlightenment and understanding is acquired. The higher man ascends, the more he realizes the beauty of perfection and the more clearly he sees inexistent GOOD as well as EVIL within it.

Then he regards the Divine as the Absolutely Beautiful, as the most Perfect of Perfection, as the most Just of Justice, as the most Beloved of Love, as the brightest of Brightness, as the most Eternal of Eternity, and as the most Blessed of Blessedness.

Every time the manmind is enlightened and spiritually elevated, every time it reacts to the rays of the Intellect, every time it feels the gentle push of the soul, it (the manmind) feels the concept of Divinity in its entirety. Then, evil is defeated, and lost, and extinguished, and forgotten by the region of the Mind. Now, the other side of this distinction is developed, the one we call good. The more the Mind develops and catches the vibrations of a superior value (intensity) of our world, the more this good – the distinction of man's most beautiful thoughts, words and actions – becomes manifest and grows to gigantic proportions.

This broadened perception of the Mind appears after man has acquired the experiences whose aim it is to help the unfolding of his Mind step by step. This ascending ladder needs great patience and persistence in order to awaken the very busy Mind within us, which is generally occupied with the events–phenomena all around nature. There are **methods**, however, which guide the manmind to find its orientation toward the **Intellect** and the **soul**.

As a first method of orientation toward the truth, we have **Metaphysical Philosophy, Esotericism** as we call it. Esotericism can bring the manmind happiness by pushing it to go through the doors of death and to enter the **Kingdom of the Heavens,** where the worlds and the souls enjoy full knowledge of the truth that is named **BLESSEDNESS....**

From death to life and from temporariness to eternity. That is what the forgotten mentor of the people, Metaphysical Truth, gives us. Esotericism takes us from evil, deceit, mortality and transfers us to the Beautiful and the True, to the Eternal Good.

I am reading my notes, which I wrote thirty years ago in
Alexandria of Egypt. Today that I am reading them again,
all these years have passed.

This memory was written in May 1955. I was forty
years old then. Now I am nearing seventy and we are in
the month of May, in the year 1985. The following is an
exact copy, without any corrections made at all.

Only a few hours have passed since I found myself
somewhere else, not naturally asleep but as if I were continuously meditating in a new way, which I just felt today,
Sunday afternoon of May 1955. The smells of the roses
and of the other flowers had stirred something within me.
It was only six in the evening when I sat down to write.
But I sat down, more to think about the mystery of Meditation and how man could convey his conscious life (the
meditator) to the capricious moments of Meditation.

In brief, my problem was whether I could meditate
and at the same time be in a conscious state, even one
slightly equivalent to the meditative state... .

This is what I had arrived at. Every day and for many
hours, I studied at what point exactly consciousness ceases dominating our Mind. Then, exactly who governs?

Who guides our selves? Does hyperconsciousness take
the reins when one descends? Or does some quality of the
subconscious that we are not aware of take over? These
were the type of questions I had when I sat to meditate. I

tried to observe matters in every detail and with unerring accuracy.

I set conditions upon my consciousness to observe and to control the phases of my experiment as much as it could. Then I asked my subconscious to help my ascent and to convey whatever it perceives to my consciousness. Finally, I appealed to my hyperconsciousness and I asked it to take over control from my conscious and subconscious as soon as I started to concentrate and to withdraw from my senses.

The reader must realize that these thoughts are written maladroitly by a researcher who is experimenting on himself. Because experiments of this kind don't take place with other people or through other people. They must be conducted directly by the researcher himself, without any other person.

After I took all these measures, I started my preparations (breathing and rhythm), going through the stages of Pranayama, Pratyahara and arriving at the legendary Dharana. Before I entered Dharana, I corrected my position always with my eyes closed and my Mind semi-thinking and semi-operating.

That's how things were when I heard the clock in the dining room strike eight-thirty in the evening. Together with the final stroke of the clock, with the time being half past eight impressed upon my mind, I quite suddenly lost control of my Mind and I entered a curious feeling.

I had the impression that I kept ascending and that the whole time, I was trying to ascend. I felt a tendency to return to the same things, but I could not do so. Something above me was pulling me or pushing me to the higher and lighter. I had the feeling that I was passing through other regions, with less air and colder. I was afraid yet I went through them. I understood nothing else. Nor did I feel anything but this constant ascent, which took me through lighter and cooler zones... .

Now, the ascent became faster and more abrupt. But I realized that my mind wasn't operating on consciousness. I realized it when I couldn't remember who I was anymore, where I had started from and what my purpose was. Everything seemed new and unfamiliar to me, as if I were being reborn somewhere else, in other life conditions and with other variables which were unknown to me.

I was truly being born in a new world that didn't look anything at all like the one I had been living in for forty entire years. At some point, it seemed to me that I collided with something and that the shell I was travelling in broke. With this contact, the shell, the egg, the hood, call it what you like, broke, and I jumped out, falling on something soft or on thinned-out cotton. I didn't feel any pain at all, nor did I worry. It seemed very natural to me to land on cotton and that the shell of the egg I was supposedly flying in cracked open.

With this impact and with the opening of my shell, it was as if my eyes opened and I began to see the strange and unintelligible things that I will narrate to you. However, I should tell you that something inside me made me throw a stealthy glance at my physical body. It was in the normal position I had left it in when I closed my physical eyes and started meditating, as I told you. Suddenly, I felt a jolt within me and I immediately orientated myself in my new state that had another body, other eyes and other features.

Now I was securely fastened and I began to gather impressions from all around me. All my senses were operating in overdrive and, in fact, at a peculiar rate of speed and depth. Many old acquaintances of mine, supposed friends and colleagues, appeared before me.

I was sitting on a seat, and as they passed before my seat, they greeted me happily and they kissed my hand, as I took off the odd hats they were wearing.

Then they moved to one side and occupied their seats, standing up not sitting down, and they didn't seem to be touching the ground but they seemed to be standing on air about 3-5 fingers above the alleged ground. As soon as they reached their area, they united their melodious voices with the others, and together with their partners, they formed a symphony that created a heavenly and super-heavenly harmony. I thought that this was normal, even my seat was normal, because now they passed before me in an orderly fashion and I stamped their cards that were folders, fastidiously noting down the hours and their subdivisions.

But I felt so good, I felt wonderful, especially with my sense of hearing, which informed me about the wonderful things that I was hearing. Now the harmony reached its peak and I was overwhelmed by the melody.

I stopped checking the cards and yielded heart and soul to the harmony that this polyphonic melody was gifting me.

Now the scenery changes. All these beings that I had seen in front of me became an instrument in my hands, which, though I could not describe it, I played it quite adeptly and this gave me the harmony of sounds that I had initially thought was being created by thousands of beings. Little by little, I become master of my instrument and I control it. I want to express as many of the heightened and pure feelings I have and possess as possible. At this very moment, my instrument takes on another shape and becomes a nice circle, whose glittering metal emits thousands of undefined colours.

My fingers pressed buttons, thousands of hand buttons that converted the sound according to the ability of the nerves in my fingers. Then, I began to produce these Divine musical sounds and to feel a Divine delight that overwhelmed me and literally melted me. Incidentally, I cast my psychic eyes all around me and I saw thousands of figures, observing me and smiling at me, as if they were old acquaintances of mine....

As time went by, my musical compositions became all the more perfect and more enthusiastic. And that's because I saw the people standing up and applauding strangely and endlessly. They didn't applaud with both hands, but with their foreheads, two people at a time or three people at a time and the happiness they felt matched the joy I saw on their ineffably happy, extremely kind faces. Now I had no musical instrument at all. This entire symphony was coming from my body.

Actually, from my mouth. Now I perceived that it didn't even come from my body or my mouth. This harmony was coming from my Mind. The Mind was emitting this harmony. Then I understood that it was my soul and that there was no Mind. In the end, I realized that it was my Spirit within me that was creating all these radiating impressions. But what were they?

When I fell down suddenly and received a strong jolt, I felt acute pain and I became scared. It was nine o'clock because the clock was striking nine times... I remained there for half an hour. I had had my most peculiar experience... Where am I, I wondered. Many years went by before I found out I had been in the highest, in our superior astral world.

Margioris: What will he write? Who are these people? Who is it? Is Ilias here?

Students: He is here.

Margioris: They are all from the **Eighth Dimension** where the **Akashic Records** are. Well, they go and read them there and they each convey them to you in their own way.

In order to supervise them, you too must go over there and read the **Archetypes,** the **Ideas** of the **Father.** But you don't have the time to go there, to ascend and so these intermediaries appear to help you, but they make great mistakes in the transfer. Did you realize that?
So, you must possess partial or general knowledge of these things and be in a position to supervise them, to receive what they read to you or what they convey to you from the Akashic Records. That is the great art of he who writes... not to fall into the trap.

Ilias Katsiampas: Does access to the Akashic Records provide access to all knowledge or on one subject alone?

Margioris: On one subject. They are immense; they are the **Archetypes.** They are the **Library** of **His Father's Darkness.**

Ilias Katsiampas: And how often may someone go?

Margioris: It is not so easy, since you are incarnated, that's why you use the intermediaries who go in order to accommodate you. But most of them make huge misinterpretations, grave errors. And you must be able to put them in their place, or being frustrated, you go and see that it isn't possible. You go and you see and you say this is not right. And do you tell him how it is? That's how I explain it. That's how I see it. Do you understand how it is?

Smaro: Just like with us, each student explains His teachings in his own way. It is the same everywhere.

Margioris: It is the same. What we discussed tonight... it will be conveyed differently by Ilias, differently by Eleni, differently by Irini, differently by Smaro, differently by Alekos, and differently by Vassilis who heard it for the first time and will say other things. That's why these things are always dangerous.

These are the mistakes they commit. Not by bad intention. Because of the formation of each person's constitution, their words.

Eleni Antoniadou: But the Master checks everything, that's the difference.

Margioris: Yes, you must able to do so, which doesn't mean that you will remain infallible and that you won't get burnt someday, but for the most part, you will be writing a reality, a controlled object....

Smaro Kosmaoglou: In other words, the most experienced soul, the oldest soul... .

Margioris: If you are older than they are, you will definitely make fewer mistakes. Since you supervise and observe them and you say to them, "Go to hell, go away." But these are high-grade details that you must find. You cannot get up all the time and submerge yourself in the Akashic Records, to waste six months ascending and descending in order to write five pages. You must be helped by them.

Anyway, errors always occur but errors shouldn't occur continuously and they shouldn't go against what is right.

Dimitris Tsaparas: Can't they transfer them, Master, from the hyperconscious to the conscious?

Margioris: No, no. They are very far away, they convey it to you from very deep inside and they change it in their own way. Some are old mystics, others are occultists, others are archangels, others are your own relatives and so on. They are a motley crew of people that bring you information.

One radio station tells us somebody set the fire, the other says that the fire started by itself, one station says there were three victims and the other says only one person was injured. And you see that ten radio stations describe the same event in a different way. It is something like that.

Ilias Katsiampas: Is their approach easier and does it take place in a shorter time?

Margioris: Yes, but they come to the astral and the mental and you meet them and you write them down. Good night. Many happy returns. Tomorrow, God willing.

Margioris: Good day.

A FEW WORDS ABOUT THE 30-DAY NIRGUNA SAMADHI-THEOSIS OF NIKOLAOS A. MARGIORIS, THE SPIRITUAL MASTER

In response to the request–question of Zezmperg, I think it would be useful if I start my introduction to the Greek public by narrating my personal perception of the spiritual experiences of Master Nikolaos A. Margioris as they were narrated to me by him.

First of all, we should point out that Master N. A. Margioris had **Esoteric Experiences** from a very young age. But his first **Complete Theosis–Enlightenment** occurred when he was **13 years old**. Throughout the course of his life, there followed **frequent Mystical Free Ascensions–Experiences** that lasted very little or even very long in earthly time, depending on the case.

But the one that lasted the longest and was richer in **Esoteric Spiritual Fullness** was the one of **nearly 30 days**, during which he not only **traversed** the **entire Esodepth of Creation**, with the assistance, the accompaniment and **guidance** of **Jesus Christ**, through whom he managed to approach the (GNOFOS) substance of the **Father**, but he also remained, on the basis of the place-time limits of the 30 days, in **constant Contact** and **the recipient** of **Supreme Knowledge** and **Wisdom** concerning the **Divine Meaning, Omnicreation, and the Superior Beings** that **Supervise** it and the **General Divine Plan** that **Guides** it and **Maintains** it **from end to end.**

During the **Full Absorption–Bedazzlement–Theosis–Communion** with **Divine Hyperrealism,** he conceived the **One Hypertruth** of **Everything** and the way in which it "disperses" Its Powers, "Exhaling" **Omnicreation,** the **Laws** by which it is Supported and the Beings that take care of it, the **Divine Order** according to Melchizedek that corresponds absolutely to the **Divine Orders** and permeates with Its Spiritual Energy, All Expression and reaches the human spiritsouls that it created in His likeness, and which have the exquisite grace of **Direct Communion** with Him, **through Jesus Christ** ("I and the Father are one", "you are my brothers, whatever I do, you can do too"), on condition that they are prepared to turn their eyes upwards toward spirituality. They will leave their ephemeral interests behind in order to find the **Unchangeable** and **Eternal Divine interests.** He managed to **Transform** all these **bright** and **sublime Meanings, Values, Virtues,** pieces of **Knowledge, Hyperlaws** and **Permanent Immovable Invisible Channels** of an **Unbroken Flow of LOVE** that **Join** the **Maker** and the **Creatures,** in a **Uniquely Full** and **Pure** way and to convey them to the expectant and restless logic so that it can conceive – as much as possible – **the Divine Events.**

At the same time, he attempted and in our opinion he succeeded – in an unprecedented way in fact – in conveying **orally** and especially in an extremely simply **written manner whole intact Parts** of the **Divine Truth** and of the **Esodimensions** to the **common experience** of **anyone** who is **interested** in order that he be informed, in great detail, about who he is, where he comes from and where he is going, what his role on Earth is, what his destination is, what his true origin is, how he can **Truly** recognize it, what means he must use, and how he will be helped in this **redefinition** of **His Being** and **His Repatriation**... in relation with the **Divine BEING**....

Of course, during these 30 days, he would return to natural consciousness for a little while, he would relieve his body of its basic needs, he would write tirelessly about **His Revelations** in his work *The Birth and Death of the Worlds and Beings* and then he would leave again....

Such **hyperevents** of **Exceptional human Beings**, who obviously have a **Special Divine Mission**, who enter a **FULL** and **EXTENDED ENLIGHTENMENT– THEOSIS**, which they even manage to **GROUND** in an **Unparalleled** and **Pure** way, using **Modern, Fully Comprehensible speech**, appear very rarely – especially in our days – and they **Call-Invite** us to **Beware** and to **study meticulously** and **critically** everything that is **Revealed** to us.

Thus, it would be wise for us to approach their Works with **sound–pure–open–critical thinking** and mainly, with **great Respect, Humility, Sincerity** and a **disposition** for **learning** and the **self-denial** of our small egos– selves....

With humble love,
Ilias Katsiampas
(Head of the Omakoios of Trikala and Thessaloniki)

SUMMARY OF MASTER N. MARGIORIS' WORK:

The Birth and Death of the Worlds and the Beings

(matter-antimatter-hypermatter, universe-antiuniverse-hyperuniverse)

So as to inform whoever is interested in *"Margioris' Apocalypse"* we quote the brief summary and the contents of his book *The Birth and Death of the Worlds and the Beings (matter-antimatter-hypermatter, universe-antiuniverse-hyperuniverse)* in which he "exhausts" within all possible human limits, for the FIRST TIME on our Planet, the Greatest Topic of all Times and Peoples of the Earth, the Eschatological issue, conveying Whole Parts of the Transcendental Divine Truth (of the Divine Plan) to our Dimension and to our three-dimensional reasoning.

The Birth and Death of the Worlds and the Beings (matter-antimatter-hypermatter, universe-antiuniverse-hyperuniverse) is the tenth of the approximately 189 books by Nikolaos A. Margioris, with the first edition in 1979 and the second edition in 1990, with complementary and explanatory material.

In this work, the author gives a completely Personal answer to the Great matter of all Times, the COSMOGONIC-ONTOGONIC and the ESCHATOLOGICAL MATTER. His mystical soul reveals its Deep Experiences and tries to give the Answer, using the Mind and the pen as a means for the hyperintellectual and the hyperconscious events. Based on these, an Eternal Creative Circle unfolds, one that is Coordinated and Created by the WORD that in our human language is called Jesus Christ.

In the said transcendental work, a Deep and Endless series of Visions prevails, combined and reinforced by Nuclear Physics, Astronomy, Astrosophy, Theology and Esoteric Philosophy, starting from the preface and arriving at the epilogue in all its immensity, offering the surprised reader some scenes of Hyper-biblical and Improbable Images.

The Birth and Death of the Worlds and the Beings (matter-antimatter-hypermatter, universe-antiuniverse-hyperuniverse) unfolds on the physical screen before the reader who follows and sees that none of the beings that are born in the various worlds of Creation are exempt from or escape the Eternal Laws that determine and direct their beginning and their end.

Matter, Antimatter and Hypermatter faithfully obey and follow the executed Plan of Him, whose purpose is the Evolution of the worlds and of the beings, the products of His Essence. An endless struggle of His divided Powers bears life and form to His infinite worlds and guides the eternal BEING. This Superb and Eternal Phase during which the First sperms of Omnicreation move, is described, interpreted and depicted elaborately on the pages of this unique book....

CONTENTS OF THE BIRTH AND DEATH OF THE WORLDS AND THE BEINGS (MATTER-ANTIMATTER-HYPERMATTER, UNIVERSE-ANTIUNIVERSE- HYPERUNIVERSE)

PART THREE OF THE 2nd EDITION

**The Interview was given in May
and has been posted since May 22, 2002**

1) Tell us a few things about yourself (a small biographical note) and your position in the Omakoios of Trikala and Thessaloniki.

I was born in 1965 in Trikala, where I grew up and I now reside. From a very young age (13 years old), I had a burning desire to learn about esoteric matters and after a five-year period with various studies at different schools, I became acquainted with the personal work of my spiritual Master **Nikolaos A. Margioris** (1913-1993).

From that moment on (1993) and in a time period of less than 4 years, I gradually acquired and I closely studied all of his **189** works in which I discovered an inexhaustible Treasure of Esoteric Knowledge that shook me up, first because it was something completely new in the Greek bibliography, and secondly because, in spite of the numerous volumes of similar books I had read from time to time, it was the first time that I saw so much accumulated KNOWLEDGE (combined with real LOVE) unravelling before my eyes, and it was given so analytically, in layman's terms and above all through the personal experiences of a true Initiate, who was in actual fact, Greek.

During that same period, I enrolled in his School (Omakoio of Athens) and participated in all the activities they offered (Metaphysical Philosophy, Esoteric Theology, Systems of Yoga, Esoteric Therapeutics, etc.) and I stayed by his side as a student until his physical end (1993). In particular, the last 4 years of his life here, I had the good fortune to be a member of his close circle and to communicate continually and directly with him, having the "special privilege–permission" to INCESSANTLY ask him persistent, unremitting questions about the deepest ontological and cosmogonical matters, to which I always received substantial, thorough, eloquent and catalytic answers.

Parts of my personal relationship with Master Nikolaos A. Margioris – as well as other details – are described in my first book with the title *From the Master's Mouth to the Student's Ear: With a thorough 400-word glossary of Sanskrit for the students of Yoga*.

In **January** of **1992**, with Master **Nikolaos A. Margioris'** permission and blessings, I founded the Esoteric School, the **Omakoio of Trikala**, which he himself inaugurated in the presence of many of his students. Since then, I tirelessly continue to open-handedly spread the knowledge and the experience that I acquired from the **Master** to whoever really wants to learn about the deepest folds of himself and of Creation, at the same time providing them with all the required practical means to use their own free will and dynamism to open the channels of communication with their inner Source of Life and of Everything.

In 1999, I extended the activities of the **Omakoio of Trikala** to Thessaloniki, where I founded the **Omakoio of Thessaloniki.**

Concerning my exoteric qualifications, I am a graduate of Physical Education and I have been working as a journalist in Trikala for 10 years.

2) What is your opinion about the founder of the Omakoio? How are his teachings different from all the other ancient and modern Masters?

Regardless of my personal view, which I will express below, if you ask anyone who is seriously occupied with esotericism for a general unbiased appraisal of N. Margioris' work, they will tell you that we are talking about a unique, dynamic, innovative **Greek presence** in the field of **Esotericism** – and not only – who undoubtedly constitutes an invaluable **ASSET** for our country and the world, in general.

My personal experience and opinion (if it is of any value) is that Nikolaos Margioris was a man who contained within him "the entire" depth of the **Occultist Greatness** of **Creation**, combined and crowned with the **Mystical Experiences** that constitute our fellow beings who are given the title of **Initiate** (occultist and mystic).

He himself in his only (first and last) interview in issue 20 (December 1992) of the metaphysical magazine "**Third Eye**" a few months before his physical death, in self-revelation, declared himself a **Christocentric and Christocratic Mystic**. The title of the article was "**The Patriarch of Greek Metaphysics**".

In any case, it should be emphasized that only personal contact with the work of the writer (189 writings in total) will provide someone with the **ESSENCE** of the person and experience of Margioris and allow him to reach his own conclusions, without being influenced by the opinions of others, including ours. I'd like to add another detail. Whatever degree of perfection is acquired in our world, however high it may be, is of "relative" value, since it is found in matter (within limits). But because it wanders about aimlessly and communicates with the eternal, it has a continuous connection with INFINITY and it never ceases to extract and ground hypersubstantial Truths that only the select VESSELS of the LORD are worthy of.

Nikolaos Margioris' teachings do not bring or promise a new type of salvation to humanity. He simply" revives" and combines, to a certain great degree, – through the personal "filter" of his actualization based on contemporary **reality** and **necessity** – ancient Greek initiation, Egyptian initiation, Hindu initiation, and finally the Christian Esoteric Initiation in a harmonious "coexistence" and a common course of possibilities and opportunities that spring from the personal need to fulfil the pursuits of every person individually.

But apart from all the aforementioned, what makes the

major difference in the teachings and in the writings of **Nikolaos A.** Margioris is that he gives a personal AN-SWER that is all **HIS OWN** on the great subject of all times, **ESCHATOLOGY** (Apocalypse N. Margioris).

His mystical soul reveals its experiences and by ap-pealing to the Mind and using the pen, it tries to provide answers about hyperintellectual and hyperconscious oc-currences. They are the basis of an eternal creative circle that is coordinated and created by the WORD (LOGOS) that in our human language is known as **Jesus Christ.**

His full **Spiritual Vision** (His Mystical Life) is set down and made public for the first time in many of his books, such as *The Birth and Death of the Worlds, Esoteric Phi-losophy, Life After Death, Creation of the Worlds*, etc. (see our site **www.omakoio.gr**), described in a way that is accessible, incomparable and contains an exhaustive source of revelations about all the stages of Creation, the Laws that govern it, the Hyperbeings that rule internally and the One Beginning-Principle of Everything. This is where the entire spiritual clew of the Genesis–Manifes-tation of Creation is unravelled along with all its phas-es–stages, its Maintenance in material form (visible and invisible) over long periods of time, the Death and the Absence of every manifestation providing a hyper-pan-oramic, UNPRECEDENTED in depth and analysis, inex-haustible PRESENT, (conceived as a UNIFORM WHOLE by a profoundly visionary fellowman–mystic in the Eter-nal Present of the One Existence of Everything), which in our humble opinion is USEFUL KNOWLEDGE for anyone who is seriously interested, whatever their beliefs and opinions.

3) Why are there so many Omakoios today in Greece? What is their relationship?

As I said before, in 1978, Master Nikolaos A. Margioris founded, for the first time in Greece, the **Omakoio of Athens** (Omakoio, Om-akouin = from the word *omou* = *together we hear elevated esoteric teachings* or *we hear the OM, the perfect sound*).

Much later and after many years of instruction, his students-staff, with his consent, founded similar neo-pythagorean practical philosophical schools, which he himself inaugurated.

More specifically, in October of 1990, the **Omakoio of Lamia** was founded and run by **Dimitris** and **Koula Tsapara** and in January of 1992, the **Omakoio of Trikala** was founded and run by **Ilias Katsiampas**. After the departure of the Master (May 1993), **Smaro Kosmaoglou**, his assistant, undertook the management of the **Omakoio of Athens**.

The three above Omakoios are self-sufficient, self-reliant and independent organizations–metaphysical schools offering a wide range of esoteric activities and, of course, each one has its own master and its own personal separate responsibility and vibrational conveyance of Esotericism.

After the transmigration of Master N. Margioris and with the passage of time, these three mother Omakoios extended their activities. Thus, the **Omakoio of Athens** branched out in **Corfu**, in **Piraeus** and in **Rhodes**. The **Omakoio of Lamia** in **Kallithea of Athens** and the **Omakoio of Trikala** in **Thessaloniki**, while his students are actively teaching in two places in **Karditsa**. Older staff members of N. Margioris have undertaken to run two more activities in **Komotini** and in **Loutraki of Corinthia**.

Finally, all the Omakoios are connected through the Liberal Pythagorean Philosophical Union in the common service of the **Testimonies** of **Nikolaos Margioris**, the spiritual Master, which combine not only his personal spiritual experiences (modern revelations of N. A. Margioris), but also antediluvian Knowledge from the East and West, which originated from the mother hearth-source, the larger area of the Mediterranean, from our ancestors the Pre-Greeks called Dravidians, who were the rivals of the Atlanteans.

4) What do you consider to be the current problems in the field of esoteric pursuits in Greece today?

Some of the problems that the field of Esotericism faces are, in general, dogmatism, intolerance, prejudice, superstition, denigration, religious fanaticism, selfishness and the general lack of basic intelligence and well-balanced emotions or the deliberate persecution by many 'experts' or non-experts of the opposing side (and many times, of our side) who willingly undertake modern "crusades" against the freedom of thought, against the dissemination of ideas and the freedom of choice, and adopt various extreme positions that divide and blackmail the emotional and spiritual world of our fellow beings. From a position of 'power', they exert unbearable and unacceptable psychological pressure on people, sowing phobias and stress, and elevating FALSE separating walls between the supposed truths and untruths. Their responsibility is IMMENSE because they psychologically violate and deliberately restrain human souls using any means, but especially by arbitrarily and ritualistically defining this as the truth, and they are ACCOUNTABLE for this because they oppress and suppress the free spiritual drive for evolution of many of our fellow beings. The Karma they acquire is extremely heavy and it will be filled to the utmost.

In addition, there are the cases of many supposed "representatives"– of themselves probably – who never chanced upon teachers, or were driven by their need for self-confirmation, or simply wanted to make easy profits by building enterprises to provide explanations and guidance for the simple problems of the very "credulous" world, managing to "exploit" it and defaming Holy Metaphysics (Esoteric Science) and its individual branches to line their pocket, inflate their ego, all at the expense of the social whole and of the Truth.

It is true that "BOUNDARIES" are required but these are not easy things at all and even if there are, to some degree, they are not easily acceptable or even perceived.

Only with the **widespread dissemination** of **ESOTERIC EDUCATION** in every direction will the defence mechanisms of our society (as well as our own) be reinforced and, with time, people will appreciate and will prefer **quality** over quantity, **knowledge** over ignorance, **experience itself** rather than blind faith, or "ready-made" semi-knowledge that leads to the deliberate deception and defamation of every sound philosophical system of high quality, native or foreign.

But the greatest problems are not solely the aforementioned, which probably come to help us, to nudge us, to wake us up, perhaps to purify us of karma. The greatest problems always stemmed, stem and will stem from within us and from what we bear within us as imperfections, bonds and attachments that we must gradually master and subjugate in order that the **LIGHT** of the soul, the Christian Conscience, the Esoteric Blissful Peace find clear ground and shine. It would be good (and true) of us to see all the other external obstacles as difficulties that bring opportunities, which the Lord takes care to place in front of us in order to release us from our own past karmic errors-burdens in order to help us take the ascending path and to creatively accelerate our esoteric progress, always assisting our fellow beings so that they too can move one step forward from where they are today.

5) Why should people study and occupy themselves with Esotericism? What would be their practical benefit?

Esotericism, or otherwise **Metaphysics**, as it is generally known, contains two significant branches. On the one hand, we have **Occultism** or **Occultology**, which deals not only with whatever has remained unexplored and unresolved by science, the daughter of Occultism, but it is also driven and conducted in the immense pulse depth of the 13 esodimensions of Omnicreation, of the 7th Founding Ray, which we belong to, from the total of 13 that the Divine Plan presented for the **Universes**. There are just as many for the **Antiuniverses**, not to mention the **Hyperuniverses**, where the Thesis-Throne of the "Immovability" of the **Father** ... (see experiential revelations of Nikolaos Margioris in his books *The Birth and Death of the Worlds*, *Esoteric Philosophy, Post-mortem Life, Esoteric Initiation, The Apocalypse of John*, and additionally, *Reincarnation, Karma, Occultism* (three volumes), *The Two-Volume Metaphysical Encyclopaedia*, 34 essays, 49 issues of the journal *Omakoio*, correspondence courses, etc.

On the other hand, we have **Mysticism** (see Nikolaos Margioris' books, *Christocentric and Christocratic Mysticism, Theurgy Teaches the Eternal Way of the Soul, Mystical Teachings* [three volumes], etc.) that is exclusively concerned with one and only matter: The unbreakable union–communion–touch between the Creator and the creature and the complete "indifference" toward any creation except **Him** Whom everything originates from, depends on and ends in.

With the above meaning, occupation with the **Esotericism** that includes these two branches is **EVERYTHING** to man because it can provide profound and extensive information on all the significant questions that concern **Ontological** and **Cosmogonic** matters (of life itself, essentially) and with time, to give him the opportunity to create, even intellectually, a representative **ESOTERIC**

IMAGE of our world (and of the esocosmos) and of the Laws that govern Creation, to help him understand the role he has and for what purpose he is here and to undertake his individual and collective responsibilities through continuous struggles with himself In order to gradually and steadily go beyond the excesses of rationality and perishability and to embrace the virtues of eternity–spirituality (hyperintellectual function of the Mind), that is, of his spiritsoul. The very Mystery of Life itself.

Only in this way will he be able to understand that he is but an actor in the centre of the stage (magic, or otherwise, a hallucination), where he must definitely perform, but it is wrong for him to identify with it and with his external self, which constitutes a reflection of this theatrical scene (acting) that we call the three-dimensional world, and which has an expiry date, as does the mummy–body we all bear.

This is his **greatest** and **most substantial** PRACTICAL BENEFIT. Of course, health and harmony in body, Mind and soul are prerequisites and are achieved according to the zeal with which one applies oneself, followed by the decision to explore the invisible, to commune with the soul, or to fully detach oneself from the karmic and reincarnating bonds, which in essence constitute the **only true salvation**, which comes from a constant self-evolution through our multifarious and multidimensional daily struggles on the "battlefield" where we endeavour to bring about the divinization-deification of human life.

6) What is the future of Esotericism in Greece and in the world?

The future of Esotericism in Greece, as in the rest of the world in general, could be defined as "positive". We can and must be optimistic because it appears that, very soon, a loosening of the very suffocating bonds of sterile dogmatism and frenzied and extreme fanaticism will take place; these will not totally eclipse, of course, but they won't have the same power and influence as today.

However, at the same time, this optimism constitutes the **REQUIREMENT** that every esotericist, **whatever his level** and **whichever country his home**, exhibit the highest possible **self-sacrifice** (self-denial) of his own being in order to convey or sow as many esoteric stimuli as possible to large masses of people and, of course, to generously provide continuous instruction and training to those who are directly interested, without sparing time, labour and the provision of knowledge. At the same time, he must not fail to continually keep in check the power of his own ego. He must find the strength, despite his inabilities and deficiencies, to constantly "break" the "barriers" standing before him, to be reborn and to inspire the people that trust him, with deeds and not only with words. Finally, without disregarding the exoteric laws and disrespecting ANY fellow being, he should pursue, at any cost, his alignment with the divine laws that as a **Divine Plan** guide all of Creation.

Only in this way do we believe that the **SUN** of **Truth** will rise somehow 'faster" and more faithfully for a large percentage of people, who, in turn, will be able to get a taste of joy and peace not only for themselves but also for the society that surrounds them, which will become all the more human in order to gradually approach its angelic side that – within the context of the recycling of the spiritual and material civilizations – will be condensed within the future marvel of the emergence of the **Third Greek–Spiritual Civilization** also known as the **Valley of Roses** (*Rosernes Dal:* 2894 AD. – 3906 AD)...*

7) Do you believe that an effort should be made to unite all the esoteric groups in Greece? If not, why not?

Theoretically, every effort to make contact (not unite) is desirable and to a certain extent, it should be pursued. Especially as concerns common goals such as achieving

---

* **Explanatory Notes about the Valley of the Roses:** The Valley of the Roses is located in the broader region of the Mediterranean Basin. It has been prophesized that at some point in the distant future (2894 AD-3906 AD) it will constitute the central cradle from which the **Third Greek-Universal Spiritual Civilization** will emerge. This was recorded as a vision-prophecy not only by Nikolaos Margioris but also by **Paul-Amadeus Dienach** (a Swiss-Austrian foreign language teacher who lived in Greece in the beginning of the 20th century and who had a vivid esoteric mystical life) in his book of the same title *The Valley of the Roses* ("*Chronicles from the Future*" by Dienach – in this edition the place name *Rosernes Dal* was used as the title) translated by Prof. George M. Papahatzis and initially published in Greek in two volumes by Vakon Publications.

However, the truth is that Heaven helps those who help themselves.

some level of "recognition" for the philosophical–metaphysical schools from the state, or having our representatives come into contact to hold discussions and exchange views, always with sincerity and mutual respect. But even this seems somehow difficult since it's not certain that we will have the desired results, or that it will prove useful, nor can we be certain of the sincerity and motives of all those involved.

The human factor and human imperfections surely contribute to this. Irrespective of one's position and role, the evolution of man is, unfortunately, not accomplished with leaps, nor of course with titles and degrees, nor with beautiful and splendid clothing and displays, nor is it closely tied with Knowledge or various forms of representations, not with small or great unions nor, of course, with any verbal acceptance of the Truth. A personal struggle of life, if not of lives, is required... on a clearly and well-defined chosen path, which every person must identify with and act on.

Our little experience, as well as the general acceptance by all those who have been involved in such contacts, substantiates the difficulty and perhaps also the "futility" of this whole matter of union. Besides, all the great Masters created their **OWN** **path toward elevation** that the smaller masters and students supported and followed. They did not unite all the individual paths into ONE but they let each individual choose whichever one was closer to and expressed his own psychosynthesis, which is something that is not likely to change in the future.

The karmic peculiarities of every people, of every nation, and of all the individual groups and subcategories start from a different point of evolution and impetus and end up at a different terminal point, higher or lower. It cannot be otherwise.

Therefore, the position of every smaller or greater holder of Esoteric Truths is to remain firm in his own vibrational output and, as a result, should produce his own 'pure' work and not combine it with the work of others, which cannot de facto have the same vibrations, the same purity, whether they have the same origin or not, greater or smaller depth and quality of teaching, and the same degree of acceptance, absorption and, especially, more or less the same degree of creative assimilation or integration of one's pursuits.

To each his own. Besides, the word Union is identified with the word Perfection–Uniqueness. Only individual examples bear within them the UNION of this kind. Its application outwards, however, is unlikely and presupposes the INTERNAL union of the whole of humanity first... which, in the meantime, will have probably followed the law of immateriality....

We think that it is a common perception that the idea of a union is rather overambitious (not to say utopian) or more precisely, an over-idealized situation that does not represent, in our opinion, reality. And if such a tendency appears, it will be mainly theoretical, very borderline, perhaps even a little experimental, and certainly without any substantial, practical purpose. We believe that if we weigh matters realistically, we will see that such an effort is not foreseen for the near or distant future nor do we think it can contribute to something specific. On the contrary, it is possible that such changes will make the existing certainties obscure and foggy or even hideous, and will actually add to the confusion that people have about Esoteric Reality, thus complicating the individualized paths and the separate representations–vibrations.

8) What is your opinion concerning the view that we should occupy ourselves only with our own Greek Tradition because that's what suits us and not with the traditions and the esotericism of other civilizations and nations?

Every person is TOTALLY FREE, from the Creator himself, to choose and occupy himself with whatever he considers useful and indispensable for himself, even if his choice proves unfortunate or wrong with hindsight.

Experience and the **free pursuit** of **Truth** are above EVERYTHING and an unalienable right of every individualized spiritsoul bestowed directly from its Creator provided, of course, that they ultimately lead to a balanced and clear personal ascending path. Otherwise, it gets lost in the quagmire of the huge metaphysical field, which just like in the exoteric society, different weeds, good and bad, gentle and wild, grow in abundance.

Our perception, as expressed and formulated in the word and in the works of **N. Margioris**, – as well as from a series of external evidence: linguistic, anthropological, archaeological, mythological, religious and metaphysical – is formulated in the theory that advocates the view that the three civilizations of the Hindu, Egyptians and Greeks (and their branches all over Earth) have a common antediluvian, and to a certain extent, postdiluvian origin from a common hearth–source whose centre is in the basin of the Mediterranean Sea. Whoever is interested will find analytical details and data in the books of Nikolaos Margioris, *Dravidians, the Ancestors of the Greeks*; *The Desymbolism of Greek Mythology*; *The Reign of Minos, the Great King of Crete*; *The Eleusinian Mysteries*; *Pythagorean Arithmosophy; The Last Day of Socrates; Pharaoh Akhenaten*, etc.

According to the above, the Greek-Prehellenic Spirit is not limited to the body of knowledge that has been salvaged thus far, or in the lost stone books of the Eleusinian Mysteries and so on, but in the Whole of **ALL** the above Civilizations that were scattered in various directions, as well as in the Esoteric dimension of Christianity. They all had a Primary Source from which they emerged and spread.

Therefore, the **Whole** of the above civilizations, the Spiritual Testimonies (theoretical and practical), and not only, constitute **OUR** tradition, the tradition of all of HUMANITY that originated from our distant ancestors (terrestrial, extra-terrestrial and hyperterrestrial) and requires profound study and consideration if we wish to find its "obscure" and original roots or at least those that are more compatible with the individualized evolutionary course of today for every one of us.

Here we deem it necessary to emphasize that he who has not communed with the spiritual knowledge of our ancestors, which was **salvaged** and has remained almost **"intact"** until today, of the main **Mystical Systems of the East** and the **West** (Hinduism, Esoteric Christianity, Orphism–Pythagoreanism–Platonism, etc.); he who was not applied himself with particular zeal to **Karma, Gnani, Bhakti, Kundalini** and **Raja Yoga** did not learn anything in this life and will fall short of true perennial **ESOTERIC** supplies (Esoteric Education) and of substantial **spiritual distinction** and **elevated orientation.** It is self-evident that his steps forward will be superficial or slow or forced and also slightly and possibly misleading. What's more, all of the above also require the **CLOSE** catalytic **relationship** between **the student** and **the master**, without which nothing really progresses in any sector of our world.

9) What is your opinion about globalization? How does it affect Esotericism and Civilisation?

Esotericism, as the word itself says, is occupied exclusively and only with the inner elements of Creation, and not with the external ones.

What we see happening all about us constitutes the accomplishment of the collective karmic command of humanity and, in general, it constitutes the fair distribution of the inner impetus of the currents of life, which clearly leads toward an opening of societies, of peoples, of religions, of nations, of economies, of civilizations, of philosophies, of sciences and of states towards each other.

So-called globalization tends, by suppressing in whatever way the steps taken by the individual and collective "ego", to follow this esoteric impulse, which, however, appears before us still in a state of immaturity or entangled in narrow minded self interests and weak efforts of manipulation by the "powerful" of the less powerful, who are definitely constructing the new karmic causes of the future of those who are responsible while at the same time releasing those suffering from old deeds.

Therefore, it bears within it the seed of truth that starts from the deepest esoteric deterministic causes, but we believe that much work and great maturity is needed on the part of the people (all of us) in order to learn to assimilate it more and more and to handle it in the most virtuous, collective, holistic and liberating way.

In this, the rearrangement of ourselves that passes through the sieve of a **Free** and **Open Esoteric Education** in every direction is of **primary importance**. For the time being, this is taking place to a very small degree and in an unsuitable way for most people, and only in the few does it find the devotion it deserves and the effect it is worthy of.

True Esotericism is not at all affected by the correctly understood Globalization nor is it touched by its bad replicas; on the contrary, it follows these events from the inside, while at the same time, it contributes and advocates the acceleration of the realization of healthy moral-spiritual bases and criteria.

10) What are the future plans of the Omakoio of Trikala and Thessaloniki?

The general orientation of the Omakoio of Trikala is to disseminate the rare wealth of the Esoteric Experiential Knowledge of **Nikolaos Margioris** (and of all the really **Great Ones** who passed from our planet and constitute high **STANDARDS**: Jesus Christ, Paul the Apostle, John the Apostle, Orpheus, Pythagoras, Plotinus, Plato, Origen, Sankara, Ramakrishna, Vivekananda, Theofilos Kairis, Akhenaton or Saint Germain, and many others) to as many strata of people as possible.

But our primary purpose is to convey our knowledge and to train whoever is truly interested and who feels close to our Philosophical orientation and wishes to receive systematic education in order that he acquire as much esoteric knowledge (esoteric pearls) as possible and numerous ways to apply them in **practice** (see works of N. Margioris: *The secret of Hatha Yoga, Kriya Yoga - A Practical Method of Psychosomatic Therapy, Karma, Raja Yoga - Elevation of the Mind from the Conscious to the Hyperconscious, Meditation, White Magic, Theurgy Teaches the Eternal Way of the Soul, Esoteric Therapeutics,* etc.) so that he may begin to reconstruct himself according to the psycho-spiritual standards of **Spiritual Excellence** and the parallel support of his fellow beings.

What we turn to as the highest AUTHORITY is the person, the work and the tangible example of our Master **Nikolaos Margioris**, whose experiential work focuses on the greatness of **Theosis**, either through **self-enlightenment**

(Meditation - Yoga - Samadhi) or through the Actualization of Divinity-Deification (Mysticism–Divine Grace).

Finally, we are open to every well-intentioned seeker who, with our help, wishes to realize a completed, dream-like and unreachable, deep gnostic trip–adventure, an individual ODYSSEY of a collective, well-balanced coexistence and coevolution in this turbulent life, where he will reconstruct himself, which, if he dares, can guide him above this life or at least bring him to a substantial CONSCIOUSNESS where nobody and nothing will be able to "touch" or alter his IMAGE about the Truth.

On our site on the Internet (**http://www.omakoio.gr**) whoever is interested may find summaries and the contents of all the **189 works** of the contemporary spiritual master **Nikolaos A. Margioris** and choose whichever one he feels may interest him. At the same time, he will have the opportunity to be informed about the Schools (Omakoios) that continue his work uninterruptedly, as well as about the **activities** they organize.

Also, we recently gave an interview that was posted on the website of Esoterica.gr (http://www.esoterica.gr/prodium/interviews/katsiaba/katsiaba.htm).

I am at your disposal for any further details or clarifications you may need.

With sincere thanks
Ilias L. Katsiampas
Head of Philosophical–Metaphysical Schools,
Yoga and Shiatsu

Omakoios of Trikala and Thessaloniki
21 Kefallinias str, 42131, Trikala, Greece
Tel & Fax: 0030-24310-75505 or mobile: 6974-580768
Website: http://www.omakoio.gr or http://omakoio.blog-
spot.com
E-mail: omakoio@omakoio.gr or omakoeio@gmail.com

P.S.: Those who are interested in Nikolaos Margioris' work, and particularly in the possibility of publishing it in the English language, are requested to communicate with **Ilias Katsiampas** at the following address: **21 Kefallinias str., 42131 Trikala, Greece**. Tel. and Fax: **0030-24310-75505** or mobile: **6974-580768**. Website: **http//www.omakoio.gr.**
E-mail: **omakoio@omakoio.gr**

SECOND INTERVIEW
WITH ILIAS L. KATSIAMPAS
ON THE WEBSITE: WWW.ESOTERICA.GR

The following interview was held on 2-6-2004 and
was posted on the Website: http:/www.esoterica.gr/
forums/topic.asp?TOPIC ID=4103

Admin
Forum Admin
Greece
1651 Messages
Sent: 02/06/2004, 19:21:59

----

*With great pleasure, we announce today the beginning of one
more "Dynamic Interview" in the Forums of ESOTERICA.gr,
this time with the* **Omakoios of Trikala and Thessaloniki!**

**We would like, at this point, to thank the Schools of
the Omakoios for their Cooperative and Generous disposition, especially the man in charge, Mr. Ilias L. Katsiampas.**
The website of the **"Omakoios of Trikala and Thessaloniki"** is at http://www.omakoio.gr, where the Members
of the Forums and our Friends and Visitors can find quite
a bit of information and illuminating material – or at any

rate, useful – concerning any question they would like to ask during this Interview.

As usual, the Interview will follow the predefined Structure and Procedure we have set up. The final questions and answers will be posted in the Hospitality room of these Dynamic Interviews under the heading "**Interviews**".

At the same time, a Discussion room will be in operation – the **present** one, that is – an open room for all Members where any questions, queries, comments, etc., can be submitted, where they will be grouped and completed by those Responsible at ESOTERICA, if needed, and the final questions will be submitted to the "**Omakoios of Trikala and Thessaloniki**".

Generally, it will be a place where a vivid, creative, polite dialogue without artificial limitations will take place with the specific Institution and where those in charge or its Members will, of course, be able to participate if they wish to.

Once again, we ask for the well-intentioned, active and fertile Cooperation of the Members of the Forums throughout the Interview. As is the case with other similar efforts of ESOTERICA, we believe that this Interview can only benefit Greek Seekers who wish, above all, to seek the Truth behind and beyond the various "Shadows" of our modern world....

We cite below a selection of useful information provided by those in Charge of this Institution.

7

INTRODUCTION TO THE LIFE AND WORK OF NIKOLAOS A. MARGIORIS, THE SPIRITUAL MASTER

THE SCHOOLS: OMAKOIO(S)

NIKOLAOS A. MARGIORIS

Nikolaos A. Margioris, the modern philosopher and spiritual Master (1913-1993) was a charismatic, talented and many-sided personality, a contemporary and rare experiential spiritual figure.

He was born in Samos in 1913 and he grew up on the island and in Alexandria of Egypt. At a young age, he was guided to India and Tibet where he stayed for about 13 years, studying the exoteric and esoteric sciences. He returned to Alexandria and he stayed there until the year 1958, when the Nasser regime ousted him, together with many other Greeks. He returned to Greece where he permanently resided in Athens, teaching uninterruptedly until his natural death in 1993.

He first established the Omakoio of Athens in Greece in 1976 in honour and for the revival of Pythagorean views.

In the fall of the year 1990, he inaugurated the **Omakoio of Lamia** of his students **Dimitris** and **Koula Tsapara,** and in January 1992, the **Omakoio of Trikala,** of his student **Ilias Katsiampas.** After his transmigration, **Smaro Kosmaoglou** assumed responsibility for the **Omakoio of Athens.** The above instructors themselves or their students or even former staff of Master Margioris established other Omakoios in different places of Greece that continue the work and the legacy of Nikolaos A. Margioris.

The teachings of N. Margioris consist of the harmonious coexistence of the ancient Greek, Egyptian and Hindu mysteries with the esoteric Christian tradition. But it is mainly filtered, revived and crowned by his deep esoteric and mystical actualization that contributes to the common "treasury" of the spirit and by his personal Revelation, his own unique testimony on the Theogony, Cosmogony *and* Ontology of Creation.

He taught uninterruptedly for a series of decades, while he wrote numerous metaphysical and practical writings, among which are: *The Birth and Death of the Worlds; Life After Death; Christocentric and Christocratic Mysticism; Patapios, the Humble Philosopher; Theurgy Teaches the Eternal Way of the Soul; The Two-Volume Metaphysical Encyclopaedia; Mystical Teachings* (three volumes); *Occultism* (three volumes); *Reincarnation; White Magic; The Chiroplastic Therapeutics of SHIATSU* (three volumes); *Psychotherapeutics without Medication; Dravidians, the Ancestors of the Greeks; Pythagorean Arithmosophy; The Desymbolism of Greek Mythology; Eleusinian Mysteries; The Secret of Hatha Yoga; Karma, the Law of Retributive Justice; Kriya Yoga – A Practical Method of Psychosomatic Therapy; Raja Yoga: Elevation of the Mind from Consciousness to Hyperconsciousness,* etc.

His teachings and most of his **189 writings** were conceived and composed through the prism of his occultist transcendental experiences as a christocentric and christocratic mysticist.

His bright and multidimensional spiritual work constitutes an invaluable, priceless **Esoteric DIAMOND–
CHAPTER** for our country and the World, coming from
one of the Greatest Spiritual Children of Greece who will
undoubtedly remain in the history of our field, unforgettable and truly beneficent.

The Omakoios of Master N. Margioris constitute Schools
that teach **Esotericism** (Occultism and Mysticism), the
Systems of Yoga, and **Esoteric Therapeutics.**

The word Omakoio is a composite of the words "omou"
(together) and "akoume" (we listen). Well, we listen to esoteric-spiritual teachings (*om akouein*: we hear the *om*, the
perfect sound).

For more information about all the writings, the work
and the Schools–Omakoios of N. Margioris, you can visit
our website (http://www.omakoio.gr) as well as read the
articles by Ilias Katsiampas at **Esoterica.gr.**

SCHOOLS IN OPERATION AT THE OMAKOIOS
OF ATHENS, LAMIA AND TRIKALA

For the purpose of informing our readers, we would like to draw their attention to the existence and operation of three Genuine and Autonomous Metaphysical Schools in Greece which fully provide the teaching of **Esotericism** (according to the works of Nikolaos A. Margioris, the spiritual Master) and **were created** and **inaugurated** by the Master himself. They are the **Omakoio of Athens**, the **Omakoio of Lamia** and the **Omakoio of Trikala**.

We mention them because all three belong to students-instructors of Master **Nikolaos A. Margioris** himself, they were established with His full consent and on his urging while he was still alive, and they follow his Spiritual Testimonies and Teachings.

Certainly, every Omakoio does not cease to constitute a Separate and Autonomous Entity–Spiritual School with its own Identity, History and Work, its own Personality and Instructor.

Meanwhile, all of them are under the Protection of the Master but also in a Pythagorean Union **(Pythagorean Contact)** among themselves, while each takes care of and serves the individualized liberal philosophical work that it has undertaken under His command.

Omakoio of Athens (Founder: Nikolaos A. Margioris)
Head Instructor: Smaro Kosmaoglou
Metaphysical Research, Yoga, Shiatsu

Omakoio of Lamia (Founder: Nikolaos A. Margioris)
-Moved to Athens and was
Renamed "Pythagorean Omakoio"-
Head Instructor: Dimitris Tsaparas
Metaphysical Research, Yoga, Shiatsu

Omakoio of Trikala (Founder: Nikolaos A. Margioris)
and Omakoio of Thessaloniki
Head Instructor: Ilias L. Katsiampas
Metaphysical Research, Yoga, Shiatsu
Website: http//www.omakoio.gr
E-mail: omakoio.@omakoio.gr

In recent years, efforts have also been made to expand the work of **N. Margioris** by operating – among other things – several branches in different places of Greece.

The **Omakoio of Athens** extended its activity to **Piraeus** with a School that is under the supervision of **Konstantinos Dimelis** and with **Anna Giavassi** now acting as an assistant. It began operation in February of 1999.

Also, in **Corfu,** a second branch is in operation under the supervision of **Ioannis Sgouros** and **Soula Pouliassi.**

From February 1999, the **Omakoio of Lamia** has been actively teaching all Esoteric subjects taught in Athens at the **Pythagorean Omakoio.**

Finally, apart from its current activities (16 years of continual and unhindered operation), in January 1999, the **Omakoio of Trikala** started, for the second time in its history, to teach – theoretically and practically – the manifold work of the Master in Thessaloniki as well, hoping to extend His voice to the second largest city and to establish the **Omakoio of Thessaloniki**. **Vana Katsiampa** is the **Assistant Instructor** of the Omakoios of Trikala and of Thessaloniki.

What's more, students from the Omakoio of Trikala have been active since October 1999 in the wider area of **Karditsa**, providing esoteric instruction at two branches–schools under the guidance of those in charge of the Omakoio of Trikala. They are: **Lefteris Tsapoulas** (Omakoio of Karditsa) and **Christos** and **Rena Karkaletsi**.

In the last few years, **more current activities** of isolated actions or in the form of **Omakoios** have been undertaken by **former students** of the **Master** and have mushroomed in several places in different parts of **Greece** (such as in **Komotini**, by **Lena Tsatsou)**, in **Corinth** as a normal School **(Omakoio of Corinth)** by **Niki Foufa – Kornaraki** and in **Athens**, in the **Chalandri** area by **Eleni Antoniadi**.

For a period of about three years, a School of **Kriya Yoga** was also in operation in **Rhodes**, under the responsibility of **Pinelopi Kaklea**.

THE NEWLY ESTABLISHED OMAKOIOS

Omakoio of Thessaloniki
Metaphysical Research, Yoga, Shiatsu
Ilias L. Katsiampas
Website: http://www.omakoio.gr
E-mail: omakoio@omakoio.gr

Omakoio of Lamia (now Pythagorean Omakoio in Athens)
Metaphysical Research, Yoga, Shiatsu
Dimitris Tsaparas

Omakoio of Corinth
Metaphysical Research, Yoga, Shiatsu
Niki Kornaraki – Foufa

Omakoio of Karditsa
Metaphysical Research, Yoga, Shiatsu
Lefteris Tsapoulas

Omakoio of Piraeus
Metaphysical Research, Yoga, Shiatsu
Kostas and Maria Dimeli, Anna Yiavassi

Omakoio of Corfu
Metaphysical Research, Yoga, Shiatsu
Yiannis Sgouros and Soula Pouliassi

QUESTIONS ASKED AT THE INTERVIEW

*"Ask the earth, the air
and the water, what secrets
they keep for you."*

amalia
Manager
Greece
5111 Messages
Sent: 09/06/2004, 14:03:37

With great pleasure, I welcome the Omakoios of Trikala and of Thessaloniki who kindly agreed to have this interview.

It took me some time to read your page in order to form an opinion about your group. Nevertheless, I may return with a new message and other questions after more careful study.

First of all, I shall pose a practical question.

I saw the part that refers to the **"esoteric key"**, a series of correspondence courses.

Because some of the information given there seems slightly out-dated (for example, the prices in drachmae, the telephone codes, etc.), and written a long time ago, I was wondering if anything has changed concerning these courses, such as the prices, the material, the way in which one can follow this course.

Especially if we take into consideration the great developments concerning the Internet in our days, I would like to ask if the material for the lessons, as well as student examinations, can be provided through the Internet.

Also, another question I had concerning these courses is whether there is a second, third, etc. cycle when one completes the first cycle of lessons in every branch. Or does one continue with another branch?

Finally, how profound are these specific cycles of correspondence courses? It is well known that Esotericism constitutes a huge field and the relative study cannot be completed in one lifetime. Therefore, if one wants to continue beyond the first 10 or 11 triads of the course, how can one do so by correspondence course? (I suppose that one can follow more than one branch at the same time).

But I would also like to ask some broader questions about the Omakoios:

• From what I saw on your website, but also from the beginning of the discussion here titled "*Interview with the Omakoios of Trikala and Thessaloniki*" – *DISCUSSION*, the Omakoio of Athens is not included. Does the latter represent a separate school? And if so, does it profess a similar interpretation of Nikolaos A. Margioris' teachings?

- I read on your website about the *"SCHOOL OF AT-MOLIQUEFACTION"* and this reminded me of the more general movement of our times towards alternative therapies and ways of life. Do you accept students who are only interested in dealing with a bodily problem? Or does this seminar constitute a part of the **whole** as far as the esoteric pursuits of a potential student are concerned?

- Finally, what is the connection between the teachings that are provided in your school and the broader social, cultural and esoteric context of humanity; that is to say, its evolutionary path? Is the teaching you provide a part of this path?

Thank you in advance for your reply to my questions.

Never accept the limits of man. Break the borders. Refuse what your eyes perceive. Die and say: "THERE IS NO DEATH!"

Patapios (pseudonym of Ilias Katsiampas)
New Member
6 Messages
Sent: 16/06/2004, 09:41:40

QUESTION:
From what I saw on your website, but also from the beginning of the discussion here titled *"Interview with the Omakoios of Trikala and Thessaloniki"* – DISCUSSION, the Omakoio of Athens is not included. Does the latter represent a separate school? And if so, does it profess a similar interpretation of Nikolaos A. Margioris' teachings?

Dear coordinator Amalia, thank you for your creative contribution to the preparation of the final questions that concern the interview with the Omakoios of Trikala and Thessaloniki.

But just to put things in order, I consider it necessary to make some clarifications. Your question concerning the Omakoio of Athens is not correct and does not correspond to what those in charge of the Omakoio of Trikala and Thessaloniki present, and it gives participants of the Forum the wrong impression.

To be more specific, the statement you made at the beginning of the question that the Omakoio of Athens is not included on the site of the Omakoio of Trikala and Thessaloniki (www.omakoio.gr) nor in the introduction of the interview with the Omakoios of Trikala and Thessaloniki is inaccurate.

By taking a closer look, you, yourself – and whoever else put forth the question – will see that exactly the opposite is true.

On said website, under the heading "Omakoio of Trikala and Thessaloniki", apart from the term "Omakoio" that I analyse at the beginning, I cite below all the Omakoios in Greece. Exactly the same happens in the introductory informative material contained in the Discussion Forum and with which the said interview starts.

Consequently, as everyone can confirm, the cause for the formulation of the specific question posed in the Forum does not correspond to the objective data that I personally record.

Besides, the relationships that govern the Omakoios are also described and the responsibility for the rendition and the interpretation of N. Margioris' teachings by every person individually is strictly personal.

With gratitude and esteem
Ilias Katsiampas
(Head of the Omakoios of Trikala and Thessaloniki)

zezmperg
Full Member
Greece
978 Messages
Sent: 16/06/2004, 11:45:42

I greet you,

I was very glad to see that this Internet domain (eso-terica.gr) is opening its gates to host different systems of philosophy and of esotericism!

All of us, more or less, **before becoming acquainted and residing herein** – had our "adventure" with the systems of eso-knowledge....

Once (1978-1979) in England, I heard the name of a modern Greek philosopher and I was surprised to hear this news from an Italian girl friend of mine ... It was during one of those afternoon get-togethers in various houses around London where we would meet to have "literary" discussions....

Thus, **NIKOS MARGIORIS**, the Great contemporary philosopher, came into my life. Then, I had believed that he had been affected by the mysticism of exotic Egypt.... But at the beginning of the 1990s, when I had the good fortune to spend a summer afternoon with him, ALL the thoughts I had about him changed.

He was slim, attractive, almost immaterialized. IF it were possible for me to see the figure of ancient Pythagoras, I am sure that N. Margioris would look like him, even in appearance!

He was not the humble one but he nearly touched the limits of the Mystics. In other words, he was the Mystic who would leave his philosophical STIGMA on the next generations as well!

Now that those who continue his work are the first generation, I would like to ask only one question, which I asked him as well. *Did he make most of his journeys in the simple way that we all know and use, or in ANOTHER WAY that only the great MYSTICS know?*

That's my question for the time being, and I would like to pay my respects to Ilias Katsiampas and certainly, to thank him for this gift he gave us that greatly reminded me of his great Master.

With regards

Patapios
New Member
6 Messages
Sent: 23/06/2004, 09:18:58

A FEW WORDS ABOUT THE 30-DAY NIRGUNA SAMADHI-THEOSIS OF NIKOLAOS A. MARGIORIS, THE SPIRITUAL MASTER

In response to the request–question of Zezmperg, I think it would be useful if I start my introduction to the Greek public by narrating my personal perception of the spiritual experiences of Master Nikolaos A. Margioris as they were narrated to me by him.

First of all, we should point out that Master N. A. Margioris had **Esoteric Experiences** from a very young age. But his first **Complete Theosis–Enlightenment** occurred when he was **13 years old**. Throughout the course of his life, there followed **frequent Mystical Free Ascensions– Experiences** that lasted very little or even very long in earthly time, depending on the case.

But the one that lasted the longest and was richer in **Esoteric Spiritual Fullness** was the one of **nearly 30 days**, during which he not only **traversed** the **entire Esodepth of Creation**, with the assistance, the accompaniment and **guidance** of **Jesus Christ**, through whom he managed to approach the (GNOFOS) substance of the **Father**, but he also remained, on the basis of the place-time limits of the 30 days, in **constant Contact** and **the recipient** of **Supreme Knowledge** and **Wisdom** concerning the **Divine Meaning**, **Omnicreation**, **and the Superior Beings** that **Supervise** it and the **General Divine Plan** that **Guides** it and **Maintains** it **from end to end.**

During the **Full Absorption–Bedazzlement–Theosis–Communion** with **Divine Hyperrealism**, he conceived the **One Hypertruth** of **Everything** and the way in which it "disperses" Its Powers, "Exhaling" **Omnicreation**, the **Laws** by which it is Supported and the Beings that take care of it, the **Divine Order** according to Melchizedek that corresponds absolutely to the **Divine Orders** and permeates with Its Spiritual Energy, All Expression and reaches the human spiritsouls that it created in His likeness, and which have the exquisite grace of **Direct Communion** with Him, **through Jesus Christ** ("I and the Father are one", "you are my brothers, whatever I do, you can do too"), on condition that they are prepared to turn their eyes upwards toward spirituality. They will leave their ephemeral interests behind in order to find the **Unchangeable** and **Eternal Divine interests.** He managed to **Transform** all these **bright** and **sublime Meanings, Values, Virtues,** pieces of **Knowledge, Hyperlaws** and **Permanent Immovable Invisible Channels** of an **Unbroken Flow of LOVE** that **Join** the **Maker** and the **Creatures**, in a **Uniquely Full** and **Pure** way and to convey them to the expectant and restless logic so that it can conceive – as much as possible – **the Divine Events.**

At the same time, he attempted and in our opinion he succeeded – in an unprecedented way in fact – in conveying **orally** and especially in an extremely simply **written manner whole intact Parts** of the **Divine Truth** and of the **Esodimensions** to the **common experience** of **anyone** who is **interested** in order that he be informed, in great detail, about who he is, where he comes from and where he is going, what his role on Earth is, what his destination is, what his true origin is, how he can **Truly** recognize it, what means he must use, and how he will be helped in this **redefinition** of **His Being** and **His Repatriation**... in relation with the **Divine BEING....**

Of course, during these 30 days, he would return to natural consciousness for a little while, he would relieve his body of its basic needs, he would write tirelessly about **His Revelations** in his work *The Birth and Death of the Worlds and Beings* and then he would leave again....

Such **hyperevents** of **Exceptional human Beings,** who obviously have a **Special Divine Mission,** who enter a **FULL** and **EXTENDED ENLIGHTENMENT–THEOSIS,** which they even manage to **GROUND** in an **Unparalleled** and **Pure** way, using **Modern, Fully Comprehensible speech,** appear very rarely – especially in our days – and they **Call-Invite** us to **Beware** and to **study meticulously** and **critically** everything that is **Revealed** to us.

Thus, it would be wise for us to approach their Works with **sound–pure–open–critical thinking** and mainly, with **great Respect, Humility, Sincerity** and a **disposition** for **learning** and the **self-denial** of our small egos–selves....

With humble love,
Ilias Katsiampas
(Head of the Omakoios of Trikala and Thessaloniki)

Lilith
Full Member
Greece
1431 Messages
Sent: 25/06/2004, 23:39:11

Good evening!

I would like to ask the Omakoio a question, but a question that I wish to simultaneously ask every school of Esoteric teaching.

In our days, we see plenty of esoteric schools being established in our country as well as internationally, each one approaching spiritual matters differently.

I have already visited some of these schools to attend a lecture or I was acquainted with people who were closer to these schools and I have had discussions with them.

I was impressed by the fact that many schools allege that they possess – exclusively or to a great degree – the key to the gate of spiritual quests, describing the others – the outsiders – as "misguided".

In fact, I distinctly remember the discussion I had with the director of some school a little while ago, who said to me:

"People must understand that these (our) teachings are the most ancient, the most suitable, the truest," etc. and therefore, anyone interested in esoteric matters should adopt this esoteric system."

In order to give my own view on this matter, I would

like to make it clear that I disagree. I believe that every seeker will find his own way, his personal way, which will talk to his heart. But on the other hand, the division into many personal–individual paths and the lack of consensus of many people around a common core is likely to prove ineffective. I believe that it is very important that there be common ground among the seekers and the best expression of this "community" is surely the existence of a group of people with superior communication skills, who, if possible, co-existed under the same roof – literally or metaphorically.

Therefore, I would like to read the Omakoio's view concerning this matter.

Patapios
New Member
6 Messages
Sent: 30/06/2004, 08:50:46

Dear Lilith,

Nobody represents the Truth exclusively. The **Truth** is hidden **within us.** We will retrieve it from within us if we are properly stimulated. In the meantime, we need the **knowledge** that is given by a **responsible person** and not by a system–philosophy–school–organization.

However, everything depends on the necessity of our own choices. Finally, **it is we** who decide about the **kind** and the quality of **experiences** we will receive and whether or not we wish to adopt them.

What we should be looking for is the **suitable person** who will **support–stimulate–teach–advise** us and who will **systematically guide** us during the **tiresome** and **laborious effort** towards **self-discovery** and discovery of the **Truth within us.**

This, however, lies with the **karma** accompanying every soul and its **real disposition** to **evolve,** whatever this decision implies.

More simply, it depends on the **idiosyncrasy** and the **choice** of **every humansoul** and on the **sincere** and **deep motives** that push it, or in contrast, on the **insincere** and **frivolous** or **self-interested** motives that drive it to "search" for desire....

Certainly, it will find the corresponding representations. Totally extroverted, pseudo-introverted or extroverted, lukewarm esoteric, mediocre, dynamic, further incising the truth, etc.

Therefore, the question is not only if they provide the basic necessities that are essentially **substantial Metaphysical Knowledge, superior practical means** and **responsible close guidance** or if they simply "inflate" the services offered cognitively, agnostically or egoistically, or if, finally, they present them as universal knowledge for all those who must definitely pass from within it... anyhow. The question is what the soul itself ultimately seeks to find and how sensitive it is to what is presented to it.

But this is related to the goals (conscious or subconscious, clear or grey) the soul itself has placed within it or has readjusted for the better (or made stagnant or worse), based on the truest or unconventional representations of Truth it receives from those responsible, or ultimately the Truths that qualitatively correspond to it and that it can accept, absorb and, in time, assimilate.

However, sometimes, the **man who has searched** must **choose** and commit himself with great fervour and zeal to following the road he considers suitable for him and to align himself with the truths revealed by all the **Great Ones** (though this does not always happen), which essentially remain unvarying and **timeless**.

For example, the **life**, the **work** and the **sacrifice** of **Jesus Christ** is a **timeless, high spiritual standard** concerning **all** of us and calling us every moment to **compare** our own personal pursuits and formed perceptions as well as our opinions and positions with any representatives of esoteric schools. How strict we will be with ourselves and with any teachers as well as the potential readjustment towards what is right depends on this comprehension.

One general weakness we have located is perhaps the fact that the deeper folds, values, essence and actions of esoteric and spiritual Knowledge are not yet sufficiently explained, analysed and made known and accessible to others.

As a result, apart from the karma that accompanies nearly everybody – common people, students and masters – the criteria set in the search and the application of the truths fall short with their partly materialistic or light esoteric pursuits and the prevailing false, insufficient or incomplete standards in the final choice of the souls.

At any rate, the presence of a Mystic, if and provided that he exists from time to time, offers us, apart from the perfect and the fullest standards of esoteric and spiritual protypes–original truths, the most vivid and timely dynamic stimuli for the understanding and the inclination toward real work for greater perception and the conquest of Esoteric Truths.

I hope that the above answer covers the questions posed.

With regards
Ilias Katsiampas

P.S. I believe that the answer to the 8th question I gave in my first interview with Esoterica.gr, though not responding to the same question and which I quoted at the beginning, is somehow enlightening. The link to the said interview is the following:

http://www.esoterica.gr/podium/interviews/katsiaba.htm

Patapios
New Member
6 Messages
Sent: 19/12/2004, 22:52:21

ANSWERS TO THE INTERVIEW
WITH THE OMAKOIOS OF TRIKALA AND THESSALONIKI
CONTINUED

Wishing to cover all the questions that dear **Amalia** as well as **Lilith** and **Zezmperg** posed at the beginning of the interview, I offer the following analytical answers.

It is true that in some parts of the site not all the necessary corrections or improvements have yet been made. But under the heading "Publications", you will find all the required changes and price adjustments in Euros for all the writings of spiritual Master Nikolaos A. Margioris and of the Omakoios of Trikala and Thessaloniki, including the Esoteric Key (8 branches of an esoteric correspondence course), the essays and the 49 issues of the magazine "Omakoio".

Delays in updating our site and making the little changes or additions that must be made from time to time may create some doubt as to their validity to those surfing our website.

In any event, for whatever clarification or question anyone may have, we are willing to answer by e-mail or by telephone.

The **material** of the **correspondence course** of the Esoteric **Key** is the **SAME** for **anyone** who is **interested**. It has been written by N. Margioris personally and it has been published in an A4 thermal-bound edition.

There are **8 branches of Esotericism** from the **13** that **Master Nikolaos Margioris** intended to write. From these, the **5 (Esoteric Philosophy, Esoteric Initiation, Meditation, Hypnotism–Orthopsychism, Scientific Spiritualism)** contain **10 lessons** each which are divided into three chapters (triads). The remaining **2 (Astrology–Astrosophy and Esoteric Therapeutics)** contain **11 lessons** (triads) each. From the last branch, the eighth **(Desymbolism)**, only the first lesson–triad has been written.

Among other writings that the spiritual Master Nikolaos A. Margioris had planned to complete, but unfortunately had no time to, are the following **5 branches** of the correspondence course: **Occultism, Mysticism, Ancient and more contemporary Mysteries, Antediluvian Civilizations, the true Esoteric Philosophy of Yoga.**

At the moment, the registration fee for one or more branches of study is **10 Euros.** Every lesson–triad costs **15 Euros.**

Anyone who is interested in following one or more branches of study in Esotericism must first submit their registration form in **print or electronically** by e-mail or by post. The student will then receive, cash on delivery, the material that was chosen, for example, the first lesson of Meditation. After the student has studied the module, s/he is obliged to submit a written answer, by post or by e-mail, to the **9 questions** found at the end of the lesson, after which s/he will receive the next lesson and so on.

This is the procedure established by Margioris, which we respect and continue.

The development of the Internet constitutes a relatively new reality that has evolved drastically in recent years. It truly opens many possibilities. Undoubtedly, at some point in the future, Master Margioris writings will be available on the Internet, provided we overcome various difficulties and reservations we may have about providing Margioris' Esoteric Key online. Furthermore, no decision has been taken by his natural heirs concerning the publication of the branches by correspondence course in conventional book form. So, at present, this is neither possible nor desirable.

Master Margioris created the correspondence courses with the ulterior purpose of enabling all those who are interested in acquiring specialized and rare condensed esoteric and spiritual knowledge but who, for various reasons, are unable to attend the Master N. Margioris' Schools–Omakoios, which are staffed by Instructors who learned in his hands and who closely follow his teachings.

Each of these branches constitutes a **turning point** in **its kind** and comprises the **cohesive** and **deeply experiential** and highly valuable and **detailed analysis** of the **Mind–soul–spirit** from the **pen** of Master **Nikolaos Margioris.**

We, as his students–instructors, promote these branches to our students and others, and with the experience and the clear personal knowledge of his teachings and his views, we believe that we are handling and supervising the whole procedure faithfully, responsibly and consistently.

All the lessons of the correspondence course represent a **chain** in the **esoteric** and **spiritual background** for all those interested from a **distance** and **our students** who, together with their **personal instruction** in our schools, not only enrich their knowledge base but have the **rare opportunity** to **ask various questions** and to **clarify many details** and **analyses** found in the courses.

However, the present sequence of all the teachings is not easily coherent, comprehensible or acceptable from the beginning because most of our fellow beings have **special interests** or **inclinations** and they seek, first of all, to conceal them without necessarily wishing to advance or complete all the lessons and the spiritual fruit contained within them.

But in reality, the **CONNECTION of all the branches of the correspondence course,** of the **oral lessons,** of the **lectures** and **of the seminars** that we teach systematically, **as well as** of the **special meetings** within a **closed circle** that every **Omakoio** organizes more or less and in which it **discloses Details** and **Knowledge** that are not always easily spread, constitute the **actual application of Esotericism** in **collective instruction.** All the above constitute a **UNIFORM Universal Reality** that acts as a **Crown of Perception** and **Forms** the **PUZZLE** of **Truth** within us.

This is **a great achievement** for those who know how to appreciate it. **Whatever experience** follows. Experience is everything in our life that guides us to evolution. Real esoteric experience, save a few exceptions, is a long way off.

True introversion is needed, a karmic **unburdening is needed**, a lot of **work** on our **inner and outer life** is needed... **Time, labour** and **sacrifices** are needed... An **iron will** is needed.... **Humility** is needed... **real perfection** is needed... **LOVE** is needed... a transfer of all false praise or esoteric conquests to the **really Great Ones,** known and unknown, and to the **One Master of Everything** is needed.

Contact with a **Master** of the **Spirit** constitutes a **rare Opportunity – the Grace** of the **Master** for every human-soul that lives on our planet. **EVERYONE can have it.** We are **not** all in the position to understand it and to embrace it, either with closed or with open eyes. The **karma** of the soul distances man and a **free will** must operate **unhindered.**

And we say all this because the **man** we consider a **Master** and perceive as an **Initiate** no longer has physical presence in this world. We say this as **a lesson** for those who consider it as such, because **ONE never** knows what one will meet on one's way (or what one meets and what one leaves behind him), coming from the **Divine Grace** that **CARES FOR ALL of us** and **mainly** for those who **work for It** and **their fellow beings.**

Apart from the correspondence course, there are **plenty of highly substantial** and **profound esoteric** and **spiritual teachings** for whoever "aspires" to follow a **practical method** of **esoteric cultivation** and **self-arousal** supported by a **complete and comprehensive model of the exoteric, esoteric** and **spiritual life** under the **guidance-instruction** of Master **N. A. Margioris'** first-generation students, who faithfully follow his method of teaching.

Among many other things that are deemed worthy of study by our neophyte students who express a strong interest in and a strong inclination for learning are the following:

Kriya Yoga (method of psychosomatic therapeutics).

Raja Yoga (elevation of the mind from the conscious to the hyperconscious).

Karma Yoga (the Yoga of all the causes and the results of selves, of others, of the world, of the universe, the yoga of the selfless service and of the pure deed).

Gnani Yoga (The Yoga of Knowledge, of philosophical training that comes from the experiences of the Great Ones and helps in the attainment of true spiritual distinction).

Bhakti Yoga (The Yoga of love of the Divine Ideal or the incarnated God).

Kundalini or Tantra Yoga (The Orthodox Yoga of the Upanishads that aims to arouse the Power crystallized within us, the Kundalini).

Esoteric Philosophy–Theology (Occultism and Mysticism: as portrayed by Nikolaos A. Margioris).

A series of Esoteric Therapeutic Systems, etc.

We wish to point out that **EVERYTHING** that concerns the **Teachings** of **Master N. Margioris**, theoretically and practically, comes from a man who grounded it himself and who transcribed it, written and orally, "to the last detail..." That is, he UNITED, metaphorically and literally, the Earth and the Sky and he HIMSELF safeguarded this Union on his own by dispersing it in every possible direction using every possible means that the end of the 20th century provided him with.

We recognize this man as a **Mystic**, not arbitrarily nor dogmatically, but after a **gruelling** and **exhausting period of cultivation** and **practice by his side.**

It is our Master, Nikolaos A. Margioris, the Master who addressed and **addresses everyone without exception,** but who is not always heard and does not occupy the minds of the many or even the few people.

He appeals to and supports **EVERYBODY** but he occupies himself with those who match his vibrations, regardless of their level of knowledge, their social position, their financial situation, their exoteric or esoteric accomplishments, their diseases, their human imperfections in mind and body and the supposed or real spiritual level of some people....

He addresses those people inside whom something... has begun to break. And not even to all of them nor to the same degree of perception and penetration. And this, of course, is not his responsibility. He said and wrote **EVERYTHING** (be it what he could and had time to and whatever is left for his students to spread). It is we who don't have the background to take in, to absorb, to combine and to assimilate some of it. But, whatever each of us manages to take and apply from **any true Master** will be of benefit for our own evolution and for the evolution of our fellow beings. Provided that we truly wish to enter the depths of **Metaphysical Truth** and to struggle for a long time with sincerity and self-denial beside a master.

Some things speak for themselves about the personality and the work of N. Margioris. Some other things are **invisible** and **unlikely** to be **perceived** even by his most experienced students–staff, though they walked, lived and struggled beside him.

Dearest friends, we clearly not only have our own personal views about who Nikolaos Margioris was in previous historical periods, but his own direct admissions that were rare occurrences but did occur from time to time... and that were catalytic for all who had "touched" him or **unpretentiously** approached him **personally** or as **family**, and **instructively–spiritually** or as a **friend**.

However, this knowledge and everything we spoke about above are not valuable because we say so. All individuals with their own critical glance, karma, course and search must find answers of this kind in time. And this, if and only if, one is interested in and is moved by any information derived from a modern Greek Master of the Spirit, accompanied by a nearly abyssal and unbelievable wealth of Testimonies (known and unknown) that he generously left behind.

Respect for the freedom and for any need a fellow being expresses or considers as their first or basic priority is taken as a given, and in keeping with the work of Nikolaos A. Margioris and his students–staff–instructors, it is considered an obligation to grant the corresponding services and accept man as he is. We don't wish to integrate anyone who has no interest in approaching, even if this were the causal nature of life.

One's occupation, for example, with **Atmoliquefaction** does not demand nor presuppose that one have esoteric concerns or pursuits or be affiliated with the general work of N. Margioris in order to benefit from an aesthetic and clearly physical method that does not cease having an impact on the health as well as the psychology of man.

Exactly **the same holds true** for the **application** of **alternative esoteric therapeutic systems** (about 30 in number) and the **undertaking – rendering of therapeutic work,** which is of a supportive character and moderates or even confronts one's karma. It presupposes the co-operation of the patient with his physician over a series of conferences for this purpose; otherwise failure is very likely. It is also connected with the question of whether it is a karmic obligatory debt or not.

If, on the other hand, one shows an interest in further pursuing the **high meaning** of the word **Yoga** and **Esoteric Philosophy,** the **way is usually open.**

Even the teaching of **Kriya Yoga** does not necessarily induct someone in the deeper meaning of the **Metaphysical Truth** of things although it gives a **first gentle nudge, instruction** and **orientation** in such a direction after it first takes care to establish and maintain **good** and **balanced psychosomatic health** as well as to cure various **physical** and **psychological problems.**

But from the moment that someone wants to begin

initiation in **Raja Yoga** (and the other important types of Yoga that were mentioned above), things drastically change. Slowly and steadily, one finds himself continuously more **informed** and **suited** to undertake the **responsibilities** that correspond to him as a **spiritual – psychic being** as well as to receive the **significant means** that will help him, as long as he uses them consistently and **systematically**, to **open** his own **doors** in **Life**, to discover the **truth within him on his own.**

Raja Yoga constitutes the most appropriate training system for **Western people** because it applies and **trains** the **cognitive** and the **volitional** aspect of people. But it still needs **thoroughly trained** and **dynamic instructors** and a **tireless will** to **absorb** all that is taught.

A **spiritual feast** gradually lies open before the eyes of the students of Raja. Along with the **inspiration** that an instructor must provide, the student must show an inclination or great interest in gradually integrating and assimilating what they are taught. These are necessary characteristics if they wish to continue and probe deeper into the esoteric perception of life.

This is where the **substantial students–seekers of expressions of Esoteric Truth** stand out. But they too have the undeniable right to make a new choice of esoteric direction as well as anything that concerns their esoteric progress, which is **their own responsibility** and depends on their interest, inclination and the consistency they show concerning all the tools they are provided with (mental activities – spiritual exercises for evolution).

If only all of us could enter a machine that would render us accomplished spiritual beings bearing Enlightenment. This cannot be done and it doesn't hold true. **Enlightenment** is provided by the **strengthening** of the **relationship among men, fellow beings** and **God** and the **personal practical intellectual work** and **spiritual exercises** that a person must do regularly and methodically.

The evolution of the souls is not in a hurry, cannot be pressured, nor imposed. It always follows **natural maturity**, which is also what nature teaches us. Everything must come in its time and in its season.

The time of the soul or of the spirit does not come at the same speed to everybody and this is a result of things related to the **karma** that accompanies every spiritsoul, the **will** to **change–reach perfection** and finally, along with the **systematic application** of the **spiritual exercises,** the **real sacrifices** made in this direction, sacrifices beyond the nice, honeyed words or the profound ideas and the testimonies of knowledge.

Evolution has patience, we don't have patience and we believe that we have learned everything because we chanced upon some books and possibly also received some instruction. If we don't stand by the side of an enlightened Master – or even his fresh students – for numerous years, we will forever bear inside us **false** and **deceptive impressions** about **ourselves** and **others**, no matter how much we polish our behaviour or use Metaphysical Knowledge that, apart from spiritual or esoteric purity, also contains quite a bit of "**rubbish**" or numerous **inaccuracies** or **fatal errors**.... or even the personal fixations of any **imperfect human mind** that functions only intellectually without ever having **experienced** the real demolition of the walls of its egoism (of its cognitive functioning) by the few **mystics** commissioned to do this or by the few students of the Masters who can play quite a dynamic role. Or, at least, to experience **the opening of new esoteric bridges** that surpass the hollowed thought of each of us... and lead to **higher experiential perceptions** and **conquests** that **truly release** man from all the **voluntary hooks** that each of us keeps for ourselves....

With all the above, I am not trying to express my personal views and beliefs. I am making every effort to bring all those who would find it of interest and value into communion with the points of view of Nikolaos Margioris.

Unquestionably, if Margioris succeeded in something, it was in the formation of a **rich bouquet of aromatic flowers** whose fragrance **permeates the spirit** of **many great men** and **women mystics** as well as the most important existent transcendental philosophical systems of esoteric development.

The **crown** of all the above is his **own spiritual experience** that constitutes **his personal Revelation** that he gifted our world as a **Truth** (we will present the first spiritual experience he had when he was 13 years old very soon).

Within these contexts, it is evident that **his work** on a **Philosophical** and **Practical Basis** is **STRONGLY** connected with the course of the evolution of every human who truly desires it.

It provides every possible and suitable means of our times in order that whoever is interested may REALIZE his role in this life and its connection with freedom, with karma, with evolution, with Truth.

He aspires to show and to reveal this concealed and not much desired truth in all its breadth and depth to all those who expect it and try to understand it and to gradually apply it in their life and – why not? – to spread it to their fellow beings.

But the main element is the practicality that is abundantly given through daily and rigorous training in CONCENTRATION and MEDITATION (Raja Yoga) that constitute the only complete practical means for the rusty hyperconsciousness of man to move and reach spiritual recognition and the fullness of truth.

Therefore, whatever our student learns within the folds of Esotericism ultimately has a positive impact on the personal, familial, social, cultural and inner life. That is, it contributes greatly to the evolution of those involved in their harmonization with their environment and their fellow beings, with the good and mainly with the mishaps of life and finally, to a profound image of all the events that surround us and demand our attention–energy to thrive....

And all the above are true provided that the student, with the assistance of his master, firmly holds the helm in the direction of this course, without turning it in other directions, as often occurs. Also, that his intentions and his motives are pure and sincere... That is, that he is truly open to the new things he is taught and to making whatever contribution to his exoteric and esoteric life.

I wish many happy and especially esoteric Feasts to all
Ilias Katsiampas
Head of Omakoios of Trikala and Thessaloniki
Website: http://www.omakoio.gr
E-mail: omakoio@omakoio.gr

SPEECH BY ILIAS KATSIAMPAS DURING THE FEAST
TO CELEBRATE THE 30 YEARS
FROM THE ESTABLISHMENT
OF THE OMAKOIO OF ATHENS
AT THE PARK HOTEL IN ATHENS, ON MAY 7TH, 2006

"The philosophical and mystical side of Master
Nikolaos A. Margioris and his spiritual work"

*Below appears the speech by Ilias Katsiampas delivered during the **Feast** to celebrate the **30 Years** from the **establishment** of the **Omakoio of Athens** that took place at The Park Hotel in Athens, on **May 7ᵗʰ, 2006**.*

*The subject of the speech that he delivered was **"The Philosophical and Mystical Side of Master Nikolaos A. Margioris and his Spiritual Work"**. And it ended with the **OPEN PROPOSAL** to support the creation of the **INSTITUTION–ACADEMY OF NIKOLAOS A. MARGIORIS**, where his already existing **189 writings**, the written works by his students that followed after his death, the activities of all His Schools as well as his literally **FLAWLESS** and real **ORAL TESTIMONIES** about numerous exoteric, esoteric and contemporary spiritual matters... will **be gathered, preserved** and **exhibited** with **infinite care**.*

[153]

With this goal in mind, the Head of the Omakoios of Trikala and Thessaloniki is open to proposals and especially to any contribution and support that could help in creating such a rare SPIRITUAL INSTITUTION that would serve as an ARK OF SPIRITUAL TESTI-MONIES of a modern Mystic who passed through our world and generously sowed the Seed of the Truth of the Spirit, our country being the springboard from which the word is spread in every direction.

*

Dear brothers and sisters, **Christ Is Risen.**
Many happy returns of the Day.
I believe that all of us agree that whatever we are and particularly whatever supreme element of goodness and kindness we have shown until today we undoubtedly owe to two basic factors: on the one hand *to the* **God** *of* **All** and, on the other hand, to our Master **Nikolaos Margioris.**

God, with **His spiritual Breath**, covers all of us without exception and He reinforces every correct step taken in Earnest in **His** direction, **He** who is behind EVERYTHING. Besides, all of us came from **Him** and we will end with **Him** in the unfathomable depths of time, we hope before the End of Time.

However, my friends, the **Master** is for us an **objective individualized three-dimensional Ray** of the **Lord** in our world that truly, theoretically and practically, gave us every meaning, every teaching, every example, every means and every spiritual standard we could use individually and collectively.

Through his profound spiritual experiences, the most supreme being his **30-day Theosis**, during which he traversed the entire **Esodepth** of **Creation** with the help, the accompaniment and the guidance of **Jesus Christ**, he was the first in our times to provide, **orally and in written form**, his own **Mystical Revelation–Perception** in a modern and simplified analytical esoteric language, in a unique and unprecedented way.

That is, he presented a complete and perfect layered **occultist** and **mystical conception** of **Creation** and **Divinity** for the information of every common man while he taught a profusion of complete practical means, **meditation and mysticism**, the self-powered opening of the spiritual path of every fellow being always under the close guidance of an experienced ally – master and under the gaze of the **All-Seeing Eye**.

His contact with the **invisible** and with **great spiritual beings** was a daily natural act that accompanied him throughout his life. For all of us who knew him, he was endowed with spiritual vision and hearing that granted him unprecedented rights and obligations and **special powers–responsibilities** that only rare beings on our planet possess and handle.

On account of the above and because he possessed the firm touch and the consistent expression of the **Christian Ray** and had personal contact with the **Divine (Gnofos) Substance**, he constitutes for us the **beginning** and the

end of our **Esoteric** and **Spiritual Education** in an incomparable way and to an unrivalled degree.

He isn't only our brother, our father, our mother, our relative, our friend, our supporter, our instructor. He is the **fully condensed spirituality** expressed in a human body that radiated and dispersed indiscriminately the fruit of the **Divine Truth** he carried within him for the benefit, the bliss, the perception, the orientation, the enlightenment and the education of each of us, without exception.

I. M. Panagiotopoulos writes that it is difficult to feel such men. They have an infinite number of people deep within them. They are not one, they are many, they are all the voices that are within them. A synopsis of humanity! Allow me to add: A synopsis of Creation....

The **Omakoio of Athens** and the **Omakoios of Lamia** and **Trikala**, to which he directly delivered personal testimonies, as well as the **staff** of the **Master** were not only **his absolutely personal** creations but his **spiritual work** as well, which was uniquely prolific in output and substance. All of us were supported, trained, taught, admonished, motivated and urged to serve his WORK, the real work of God and His firstborn Son, **Jesus Christ.**

What we struggle for, what counts, what deserves and qualifies for eternity is always the esoteric, what is within. And this will always represent the greatest, truest and most inalterable reformation of man himself. His spiritual recognition, his spiritual rebirth in eternity.

Today's feast is the Master's feast. A feast of **Pythagorean union of all of us** to **HIM** as **He** comprises the

Top and the **Whole** of the **Work**. The connecting channel with the **Divine Source**. The **unique** and **irreplaceable point** of our transcendent congruity to the one spiritual **Hearth Ray** of the **Source** of the **Infinite Divine Light**.

On every great collective gathering – feast like today's, it is **desirable** *and* **useful** for each of us to review our progress in deeds and in character. To record the results of whichever course we have taken, to report what we envision for the future and to bring, as much as possible, the **Master** and **His work** to the **new generation**, which is making its presence felt in the esoteric pursuit.

Personally, apart from the presence of the **esoteric standard** that constitutes the central idea of the **spiritual identity** of the **Master**, I choose to refer to an extremely important matter that concerns **his Titanic spiritual work**, which contains **189 esoteric writings** and a **literally INFINITE wealth of oral spiritual testimonies.**

Dear brothers and sisters, in time, we, who are somewhat older, the students of the first generation, will recede. Our staff, our students, the next generation will take the reins, as has already happened with the second-generation students and the newly established Omakoios and their staff, as well as the others that are destined to come.

Progressively, the work will begin to undergo a gradual decline and the output of spiritual knowledge will shrink due to the distance from the physical contact with the **direct truths** and **acts** from the **Mouth** of the **Master**, from the people who knew him and met him and from the folds of his teachings that even today, as we are talking are not totally known, explicable and clear or easily comprehensible, assimilated and applicable.

The **spiritual experiential wealth** of the **Master**, framed in **love, sacrifice** and **humbleness** is spontaneous, inexhaustible, timeless, original, saving and redemptory for the souls that search for it and sincerely try to embody it.

Besides, it is not at all far from the truth that if we could capture the entire body of the Master's oral spiritual testimonies in the written word, the writings that we would present might surpass the 3000 and more books that **Adamantius Origen** is estimated to have written. And we say this with full knowledge and without exaggeration. Definitely, if God wishes, this may be achieved to some extent.

Therefore, along with today's personal introspection and reckoning of the fruit of our labour, what we have succeeded for **ourselves** and **for others**, let us speculate how we could **better preserve** this **monumental written** and **MAINLY oral work of his**. That is, how we could **honour** his **memory** and safe guard **his enormous spiritual testimony over time** on a practical level and make it more **widely** known in an **OBJECTIVE** manner, regardless of the existence or not of the Omakoios of today and of the future that, with the assistance of their staff, have the main responsibility for this work.

Questions that may preoccupy many of us and to which we must all provide an answer to ourselves, to the Master and to the Work.

We **strongly believe** that if we all participate in creating a new modern **SPIRITUAL ARK** for the collection, preservation, storage and display of the **life** and the **influential spiritual testimonies** of our **Master**, we shall make great strides in actualizing such a **VISION** that will reflect the **size** and the **prestige** of the **Uniting Vibration** of the **Master** and creating a **sweet spiritual OASIS** where the souls that need to can quench their thirst and be guided toward **perpetuity.**

According to the **Manual-Guide** for **staff and instructors of Esotericism**, the work of our Master that **the Omakoio of Trikala** and of **Thessaloniki** published in **2002** – among others – a **proposal-invitation** is set forth that concerns **ALL OF US** and whose aim it is to make the creation of the **ESTABLISHMENT – ACADEMY OF NIKOLAOS A. MARGIORIS** a **common pursuit** of the present and the future so that it can advance.

Such an action will undoubtedly constitute a **Timeless Crossroads**, a **Timeless MONUMENT** where there will be the perpetual collection, transcription, filing, preservation and **methodical promotion** (in and out of Greece) **of all** the **written** and a part of the **oral work** of the **Master** that will, of course, be readily available; of the activities **of ALL** the **Omakoios** and **their staff;** of present and future editions; and whatever refers to all the above.

What is needed **first** is **our unanimous support** and **iron will** for the accomplishment of the goal to **save** and **perpetuate** these **hypersubstantial truths** beyond the bounds of our own personalities – which according to the laws of nature will be lost – and beyond the borders of our country.

Imagine us in ten years' time or more gathering once more to celebrate the Master and being able to offer him this **gift**.

Duty always calls us, not only individually, not only personally, not only collectively, but **United** and **Transcendentally** to **Converge** with the **MASTER,** and this may be an additional concern for Him. **THE PRIMARY concern for HIM.** The concern over the continuation of his work **ABOVE** our own persons and deeds since he is the **CENTRAL Person–Deed** that contains all of us, the expression of a **Divine Spiritual Ray** in our world as a **Christocentric and Christocratic Mysticist.**

Our unshakable personal belief is that, in this way, not only will the **Work** of the **Master** and of the **Omakoios and** the **actual Pythagorean Union to HIM** be served **More Broadly Over Time** but we shall stand as more worthy of the circumstances before this **BEING** that by **Divine Grace** happened to cross our path and take us under his wings, teaching us only the Truth.

Let us truly honour this truth, this mission, this person, **this FEAST** and let us be its real carriers and tireless and humble workers.

NIKOLAOS MARGIORIS INSTITUTION – ACADEMY constitutes a **REFUGE of transcendent life** for the **future generations... It is our obligation to keep His voice alive** ... as well as **every fold and extension of His work through the Omakoios... and** their **staff....**

With the establishment of a **self-supported** and **self-sufficient Nikolaos Margioris Academy-Institution**, whenever this may be realized, and with the creation of **HIS** first **FUNDAMENTAL ARCHIVE**, I am at your service to provide material that concerns the spiritual testimonies of our Master.

I strongly believe that this institution can constitute the **amaranth Garland**, the **Olive Branch** of **his victory**, the victory of our constant and natural adhesion to **Him**, to an existent physical ending, to a physical institution that will **forever house HIS LIVING VOICE, HIS LIVING HISTORICAL ACTIVITY**, a **PRESERVED** spiritual **heritage**, to a **Central Substantial VISION of ALL of us** for the **Master** and the **future generations**, which, however, we must **DIRECTLY target** so that at some moment we can pass it on to our fellow beings and gradually, humanity....

From the depth of our hearts we thank you for **EVERYTHING**, Master.

May we be worthy of your confidence and of your blessing. Amen.

I wish you Many Happy Returns of the day, full of Spirituality and Benefaction.

Christ is Risen.

EPILOGUE

Instead of an epilogue, the Omakoios of Trikala and Thessaloniki would like to clarify that by rigorously following the Liberal Philosophical – Transcendental Work of **Nikolaos A. Margioris**, the spiritual Experiential Master, as well as his teaching methods that they consider invaluable, they will always try to emphasize as many folds of the personality and of the rich spiritual work of Master Nikolaos Margioris as possible, demonstrating the significance of his benefaction and updating subjects and answers on numerous esoteric and mystical matters that are not only little known, but are, in fact, very rarely discovered as information or they lack definite and clear answers.

At the same time, wherever it is deemed necessary, they seek, they learn, they hold discussions and commune with the experiences of our fellow beings, conducting comparative studies and applying their own approach, assessing and classifying (according to their estimation) the esoteric experiences so that if they judge them to be healthy and truly experiential spiritual nuggets, they can record them and preserve them.

In many cases, the carefully prepared disclosure of the personal experiences as well as of personal discussions between the Master and the students is extremely useful and beneficial for the newer students as well as for every researcher or student of Esotericism and perhaps, in the future, the present endeavour may be further pursued.

The reasons are many and important, some of which we include:

1) Because metaphysical and particularly spiritual experiences are very RARE and even more rarely become known. The reader who attempts to find written accounts of deeper experiences of spiritual content will see how true this is.

2) Even when such experiences are found from time to time, they are usually incomplete (and of little value) or, for various reasons, they are not communicated outwards or they are not preserved in writing so as to be classified and included in the archives which contain a wealth of spiritually grounded experiences made public in the "treasury" of evolved humanity, accessible to any interested individual wishing to comprehend them.

3) We consider it our obligation to the One Beginning of All and to the Truth as it was expressed by our Master – and of course to the best of our abilities – to gather, classify and preserve "everything" that we consider, even personally, to be important as a testimony of a psychic–spiritual experience that comes from our Master as well as from every true Master of the spirit.

4) Our personal findings, particularly in relation with the highly descriptive meanings and experiences that touch the Triadic Expression of God and of the partial details that are contained in the **Revelation** of **Nikolaos**

A. **Margioris** in his book *The Birth and Death of the Worlds and Beings*, etc., reinforce our obligation to safeguard the testimonies of His experiences that can provide unbelievable information about the **Divine Darkness** and **Its Creation** to everyone who sincerely seeks this knowledge.

5) Through every genuine spiritual Experience, a unique opportunity is provided for every self-proclaimed metaphysicist (who truly approaches it) who at some point considered himself to be something special in relation to his other fellow beings – metaphysicists or not – to revert to humility, to simplicity and to the Esoteric Truth beyond the human embellishments and idealizations.

6) Finally, any fake experiences or imaginative imitations based on the unreal quickly collapse and are denuded when they are compared with the real spiritual ones or with the people who experienced them. Especially when those who have these experiences happen to still be alive (or representatives of those who lived and matured by their side) and they relate these experiences to the point of "exhaustion" whenever there is an opportunity to hold a sincere discussion or receive instruction through a continuous flow of new details and disclosures about their experiences and their Revelations.

7) Finally, we must stress that for an initiate (occultist and mystic) like Nikolaos Margioris, everything shows

that within him shines the **ever-glowing Light** of the **One** and at the same time of the **Triadic Truth** that he open-handedly shares with everyone he chances upon on his path with great love, interest and care.

8) And for all the above, we are **ALWAYS** guided by the **Original Bright Spiritual Experience** and the **Discovered Esoteric Pearls** of our Master **Nikolaos A. Margioris** and our long-lasting service beside him that **ALWAYS** provides us with the rare ability to clearly distinguish with certainty the difference between superficial, esoteric and spiritual experiences.

CURRICULUM VITAE OF ILIAS KATSIAMPAS

Author, Ilias L. Katsiampas

Ilias L. Katsiampas was born on October 30th 1965 in Trikala of Thessaly (Greece) where he grew up and lives today. He is a graduate of Physical Education (TEFAA), he has worked as a journalist for the last twenty-two years and he is the writer and publisher of 15 philosophical works. He is married to Sofia A. Skoumi, with whom he has two children, Lampros and Maria.

From a very young age, he expressed a strong esoteric interest in seeking the essence of things, the real meaning of life. He studied many philosophical systems as well as volumes of books on Esotericism of every kind, from different times and countries, until he met **Nikolaos A. Margioris**, the **Greek Master** of **Esotericism** (1913-1993), in whose spiritual work he recognized the presence of substantial Knowledge, the supreme real truth. He became his student and remained close to him from 1983 until his physical passing on May 6ᵗʰ 1993.

Among other things, he received training in the pure form of Raja Yoga and in numerous other esoteric fields of interest (Esoteric Philosophy, Esoteric Theology, Mysticism, Astrology-Astrosophy, Hypnotism-Orthopsychism, Scientific Spiritualism, Esoteric Therapeutics, etc.) and gradually ascended the steps of his spiritual evolution.

The fiery and indomitable tendency and willingness of the writer to explore the Beyond in combination with his extensive training, apprenticeship and direct close relationship with his Master, N. Margioris for almost a decade contributed decisively to the gradual formation of his clear integrated experiential perception-point of view on the whole field of Metaphysics, as well as on the practices of meditation and mysticism.

On **January 18, 1992,** with the full encouragement, guidance and in the presence of his Master, he inaugurated the **Omakoio of Trikala**, an educational-spiritual centre, where all the **Yoga** systems (Mantram, Kriya, Raja, Karma, Jnani, Bhakti, Kundalini, Sahaja, Atmoliquefaction), **Esoteric Philosophy, Alternative** and **Esoteric Therapeutics** and generally **Esotericism** (Occultism and Mysticism) are taught to this day.

Since 1999, he has been active in the **Omakoio of Thessaloniki.**

In **July 2012,** along with his partners and students, he established the Association **"YOGA ACADEMY OF NIKOLAOS MARGIORIS-OMAKOIO"** as a tribute to his Master, **N. Margioris**, for a more holistic application of his philosophical and practical work.

He proclaims and highlights the paramount need for the widespread teaching of **Esotericism** (Introversion – Self-Knowledge) in order to create healthy and balanced minds and a truly New Spiritual Man characterized by self-awareness, self-reliance, autonomy, an open mind, a giving disposition free of materialistic pettiness and repressed desires, and an ability to better adapt and respond to the challenges of modern reality as well as to every future time of Humanity.

BIOGRAPHICAL NOTE OF
NIKOLAOS A. MARGIORIS

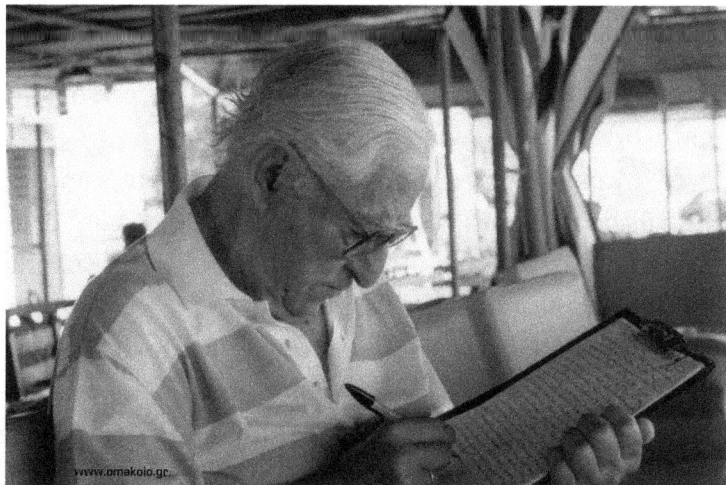

Nikolaos A. Margioris (15/12/1913 - 6/5/1993) constitutes one of the greatest and most prominent figures in the area of Esotericism (Occultism and Mysticism). He is not only a recognized, but a fully-experienced Metaphysical Omni-Scientist-Master who was characterized as 'the Patriarch of Greek Occultism' in a relevant interview of the journal *Third Eye*, in its December 1992 issue. This was his first and his last public appearance.

Therefore, this is in memory of Nikolaos Margioris, who was a great Christocentric and Christocratic Mystic and modern Initiate, and we, a group of his closest students who followed him the last few years and were lucky enough to be taught the deep elements and aspects of the Universal Truth, to enrich our Occultist and Mystic Knowledge and to receive a part of the abundant LIGHT that he spread around him, feeling gratitude and sincere, not fanatic, Love for him would like to inform every seeker of the Truth, about the Master's life, personality and work.

Nikolaos Margioris was born on the island of Samos in the village of Vourliotes on the 15th of December, 1913. When he was 13 years old, he attained Samadhi-Enlightenment for the first time.

He was educated in India and in Tibet for almost 13 years. He lived with his relatives for many years in Alexandria of Egypt where he pursued his studies and made his career. He married Laitsa Papandreou with whom he had two children, Andreas and Kalia. He fought in World War II as a reserve officer in the Sahara Desert where he was wounded in El Alamein and in Rimini. For his services to the country, he was honored with many medals (among them the Big Cross) and with a veteran's disability pension. Also, he was honored twice with the Cross of Saint Mark for his contribution to the Church by Christoforos and Nikolaos the 6th, Patriarchs of Alexandria.

Apart from Egypt, he also taught in Greece from the first day of his arrival in 1958 until 1993, when he departed. He wrote books and essays, he circulated a journal and he created a cycle of studies by correspondence courses.

He considered Metaphysics to be the only Truth and

believed that man can attain Truth as Socrates did through his famous MEDITATION (DHARANA-CONCENTRA-TION) or through Religious Mysticism (Christocentric and Christocratic Mysticism).

All his teachings, his books, his essays, his studies in Esotericism come and emanate from his deep Mystical experiences (Nirguna Samadhi-Theosis).

Since he was very young, he was a participant in these transcendental states which he managed to transform in an incomparable way and to convey to his students and to the world as Knowledge, advice, guidance, for use, practice, training, therapy and personal experience.

His philosophical approaches on Creation, on Truth (God), on the visible, perceptible and invisible, imperceptible Laws that rule the World and life, in general, are expressed with unique fluency, detail, analysis and depth. He also unveiled new Esoteric Revelations as well as presented for the first time a complete and sound Occultist and Mystic view of the Creation of All, using a torrential and overwhelming form of oral and written expression which rivals, without exaggeration – for anybody who knows – that of Paul the Apostle, Vivekananda and Pythagoras, whom no obstacle, sickness, or anything else restrained (he came close to death at least three times).

On the contrary, he believed in the provision of Everything in full, of continuous guidance, instruction and unceasing Sacrifice and the Exemplification of a prototype that can be described in two words "PERFECT MAN AND PERFECT GOD" without publicity, propaganda and proselytism. And certainly with absolute respect for the freedom of every potential seeker.

He was a faithful soldier of our Lord Jesus Christ, a 'TRUE RAVI-CHRIST' and also His imitator, having always followed His Work and His Teachings, reviving it once more in our society of today.

A few words about his multi-dimensional work
After 23 years of Metaphysical publications (1970-1993), he wrote 33 books of clearly Esoteric subject-matter. He also published 33 special essays on different esoteric matters and circulated the first purely metaphysical journal *Omakoio* in our country which included incredible and unprecedented Metaphysical analyses and helped popularize the subject.

He created a field of studies through correspondence courses under the name 'Esoteric Key'. In this field, the students received instruction characterized by a deep, theoretical and practical Esoteric analysis in the following courses: MEDITATION, HYPNOTISM, ORTHOPSYCHISM, ESOTERIC PHILOSOPHY, ESOTERIC THERAPEUTICS, ASTROLOGY-ASTROSOPHY, ESOTERIC INITIATION, SCIENTIFIC SPIRITUALISM, DESYMBOLISM.

Every three months, he held seminars in SHIATSU lasting for many days in which he himself not only taught SHIATSU but a lot of other Esoteric therapeutic systems among which were also his own discoveries whose therapeutic potential is immense and whose success rate surpasses 80%.

Some of his own discoveries which he obtained through personal experience and deep Esoteric Knowledge are mentioned in his books and were taught to his students. They are:

From the LEFT PALM of the hand, he identified the main terminals of certain internal organs of the human body. (N. Margioris' Discovery).

FINGERTAPPING: It is a rapid method of stimulating the whole organism, the cells and the endocrine glands to secrete new hormones and heal the ailing person. (N. Margioris' Discovery).

GLOSSOTHERAPY (TONGUE THERAPY): With special kneading, pulling and massage movements on the tongue that have an immediate effect on the muscular and nervous system and on the whole organism for recovery and therapy. (N. Margioris' Discovery)

HE REVIVED and used the ancient Greek Asclepean kneading-massage method that Asclepius, the father of Medicine, invented and applied in ancient times in the Holy Sanatoriums of Ancient Greece (*Asklepiaia and Amfiaraeia*).

SUGGESTIVE THERAPY through heterosuggestion or autosuggestion. Revival and presentation by N. Margioris.

SLEEP THERAPY or otherwise Hypnotism-Orthopsy-chism or Technical Sleep - three scientifically complete methods. Presentation by N.A. Margioris.

RELIGIOUS EMOTIONAL REQUEST by the side of the patient. Presentation by N. Margioris.

JAPANESE SHIATSU - Fingertapping (classification of Shiatsu by Master Nikolaos N. Margioris. 186 diseases are classified into 23 groups, each with their general as well as individualized therapeutic methods). Classification and Presentation by N. Margioris.

METHODICAL STIMULATION of all the Endocrine Glands (chakras) for remedy. Nikolaos A. Margioris' method.

BIOENERGETIC INFLUENCE on the 33 vertebrae of the vertebral column for the therapy of 193 diseases of the human body. N. Margioris' method.

STATIC Therapy with the hands-palms. N. Margioris' presentation.

KINETICS Therapy with the hands-palms. N. Margioris' presentation.

REFLEXOLOGY or reflexive zonotherapy. N. Margioris' presentation.

ICONOPLASTIC therapy from near or far. N. Margioris' method.

HECTOPLASMATIC EXHALATIONS OR HECTOPLAS-MATIC EFFUSIONS - N. Margioris' method.

MANTRAMOTHERAPEUTICS. Remedy with Power words. Presentation by N. Margioris.

TRANSFUSION OF ENERGY, healthy vibrations. Presentation by Master N.A. Margioris.

ATTENDANCE of Litanies or Liturgies.

HOLY ZEAL. The reinforcement of unshakeable Faith in any Ideal or Belief that vibrates man internally and creates the preconditions for the elevation of his vibrations in order to restore his health.

KRIYA YOGA. Method of Somatopsychical Therapeutics. It contains physical exercises-postures in combination with special breathing exercises for the revival - remedy of the body and mental exercises of comparison for the release of man from every kind of repressed emotions, phobias, passions, etc. Revival and Presentation on a universal level by Master N.A.Margioris.

KUNDALINOTHERAPY. Through the exhalations of Kundalini or/and by its awakening.

RAJA YOGA, 8 stages-steps of therapy of the body and of the Mind (scientific-psychological method).

Ethicoplasm of man, therapeutic positions according to the problem, manipulating universal energy (prana) and supplying it to the organism through proper rhythmical breathing for prevention or therapy, retaining the life force that we have within us and preventing its purposeless waste, directing it toward higher purposes, steady concentration on one and only thought-target-ideal for 12", its extension to 144" (meditation, internal identification with the target) and, finally, with the extension of the sole-thought for 1728" we come to the complete therapy of body and Mind, the Union-Enlightenment-Harmony, Full Consciousness of man.

MIXTURE-COMBINATION of many of the above Systems.

These are some of the most important, effective yet innocuous Esoteric - Physiotherapeutic Systems, some of which have been scientifically validated and are taught in universities abroad, while many others are being studied for the positive effects they have on the human organism.

Apart from teaching the Therapeutic Systems, he used to provide therapy, as did those of his students who had been trained. At the same time, he operated a school of KRIYA YOGA where instruction was undertaken by the first female teacher of Kriya in Greece, Mrs. Smaro Kosmaoglou, who had been instructed by Master Margioris himself. He also ran a weight loss school using the system of Atmoliquefaction (his own invention).

He also taught the Genuine and Complete RAJA YOGA, as well as all the systems of YOGA: Hatha, Kriya, Mantra, Karma, Bhakti, Jnani, Tantra (Kundalini), as well as ESOTERIC PHILOSOPHY - THEOLOGY, KABBALAH and ESOTERICISM (OCCULTISM AND MYSTICISM).

He did all his teaching and other activities from his seat in the Spiritual Philosophic Laboratory which was established in 1976 and was called "OMAKOIO OF ATHENS", in memory of the OMAKOIO that Pythagoras created for the first time in Croton of South Italy.

In 1972, he founded the Association "THE PIOUS PILGRIMS OF THE UNBUILT LIGHT, ST. PATAPIOS", where he regularly delivered free lectures on various Esoteric topics.

He was a Permanent and Indefatigable Worker and Guide of the Good and Perfect, a Continuous and Inexhaustible Source of Divine Knowledge.

The above are written as the smallest homage that we, his students, could render him, promising to continue and spread the legacy he left us.

NOTE: The above presentation of Master Nikolaos A. Margioris' personality, life and work was written by his student, Ilias L. Katsiampas (on behalf of all the students he taught during the last decade).

In the beginning, the Master's biography was sent, on the writer's initiative, to foreign guides of metaphysical organizations and to different other metaphysical movements abroad. Then, after the Master's death, it was revised and completed correctly by his student and the writer of this book and it was published for the first time in the metaphysical journal *Third Eye* in issue 28 of September 1993, four months after his departure.

Afterwards, it was included in the 3rd Volume of the Master's work *Mystical Teachings* that was published in 1994, as well as in the republished editions of the books *The Other View of Erich Von Daniken's Dogma* and *Dravidians, the Ancestors of the Greeks*, *The Secret of Hatha Yoga*, *The Reign of Minos, the Great King of Crete* and *The Chiroplastic Theurapeutics of SHIATSU, VOLUME 3*.

SYNOPSIS OF THE RARE GREATNESS
OF THE MASTER

Master Nikolaos A. Margioris was an Occultist (Occultologist), a Christocentric and Christocratic Mystic, a Modern, Genuine Initiate and Spiritualist.

He is the Master of Masters who silently, prudently and with unprecedented Convergence – Unity – Homogeneity of Work, Autogenous Perfection and a Uniqueness of Revelation and Rendition, exposed to the eyes of his students and to the common experience of every seeker as well as to the whole world (Esotericism for All) the Hyperintellectual (Spiritual) COMPLETE and Perfect Mystic Experiences – Messages of his Soul, his Spirit, of the Source-Truth-God itself, through his 189 books and his teachings.

We could say that the person of Master Nikolaos A. Margioris can be "summarized" in a few words in the following definition:

We are talking about the Greatest (extremely Rare) Esoteric and Greek-orthodox Radiating Personality of such Grandeur, Range, Caliber and prolificity, a creator of a Concise and Pure Spiritual Work that seems to be unprecedented and incomparable in our days, not only for Greek standards but also on a Universal level.

Were someone to attempt to "capture" in written word his preserved oral traditions and his extensive "inexhaustible" dialogues that only we, some of his students of the last decade, know, they would easily surpass the 1000 Substantial Esoteric Works (most of them expressed for the first time and revelatory in nature).

Certainly, were we also to calculate what has not been preserved or what we could not trace or other oral deliveries whose fate we are ignorant of (in Greece or in Alexandria where he lived for many years), then, of course, they are countless (they may surpass the 5000 spiritual works; the number of works that Orighenis is said to have written).

We are certain that future generations will search with particular fervor, persistence, care and difficulty for evidence, fragments, aspects and details of the person and the work of a True Modern Initiate who walked among us and who was SO giving that ultimately the people of the future, being more mature spiritually, will recognize, will "worship" and will follow with great zeal and a feeling of real respect and duty.

The reader can find some information about his person in the only public interview he agreed to five months before his passing, in the metaphysical journal *Third Eye*, issue no. 28, December 1992, where he revealed himself in public.

He who is interested will find two more presentations-reports of his life and his work in some recordings made by the narrow circle of his students in the *Third Eye*, September 1993, issue 28 (it is published above) and May 1994, issue 35. Some of them are also re-published in his books that were re-edited.

In the book of the director of the Omakoio of Trikala under the title *From the Master's Mouth to the Student's Ear, with a thorough glossary of Sanskrit (philosophical dictionary of 400 words) for the students of Yoga and of Esotericism* one can find all the above presentations as well as a more recent one.

Finally, in the 3rd Volume of *Occultism*, an important new presentation about the Master is included.

His student, Ilias L. Katsiampas, is working on a more extensive and complete presentation of the life, the personality and the work of the Master that will include even more aspects of his passage through our world and his Esoteric Work that he left as a legacy of Knowledge and Instruction for the future generations who will evolve within the framework of Mysticism (Philosophical, Gnostic and Religious).

SCHOOLS IN OPERATION AT THE OMAKOIOS
OF ATHENS, LAMIA
AND TRIKALA

For the purpose of informing our readers, we would like to draw their attention to the existence and operation of three Genuine and Autonomous Metaphysical Schools (with an extensive didactic curriculum on Esotericism) which were created in Greece and inaugurated by the Master himself. They are the **Omakoio of Athens**, the **Omakoio of Lamia** and the **Omakoio of Trikala.**

We mention them because all three belong to Master Nikolaos A. Margioris' students-instructors, they were established with his full consent and at his urging while he was still alive, and they follow his Spiritual Legacy and Teachings.

Certainly, every Omakoio always constitutes a Separate and Autonomous Entity-Spiritual School with its own Identity-History and Work and with its own Personality and Instructor. At the same time, all of them are under the Protection of the Master but also in a Pythagorean Union **(Pythagorean Contact)** among themselves, while each takes care of and serves the individualized liberal philosophical work that it has undertaken under His command.

OMAKOIO OF ATHENS
SMARO I. KOSMAOGLOU
METAPHYSICAL STUDIES IN YOGA AND SHIATSU
ATHENS, GREECE

OMAKOIO OF LAMIA
DIMITRIS & KULA TSAPARA
METAPHYSICAL STUDIES IN YOGA AND SHIATSU
LAMIA, GREECE

OMAKOIO OF TRIKALA
ILIAS L. KATSIAMPAS
METAPHYSICAL STUDIES IN YOGA AND SHIATSU
21 KEFALLINIAS STREET
42131 TRIKALA, GREECE
TEL. & FAX: 0030-24310-75505 & MOBILE: 0030-
6974-580768
Website: http://www.omakoio.gr
E-mails: omakoio@omakoio.gr & omakoeio@gmail.
com

Recently, individual efforts are also being expended to make His Work more widely known with the operation – apart from everything else – of new branches in various parts of Greece.

The Omakoio of Athens is extending its activities to Piraeus with a branch that will be under the supervision of Konstantinos Dimelis and which will start with the instruction of the Esoteric Philosophy of the Master and Kriya Yoga.

Also, a second branch is already in operation in Kerkyra (Corfu) under the direction of Ioannis Sgouros and Soula Pouliassi, where Esoteric Philosophy, Esoteric Therapeutics and Kriya Yoga are being taught.

The Omakoio of Lamia is expected to extend operations to Kallithea, in Athens.

Finally, the Omakoio of Trikala, apart from its current activities (with 8 years of continual and unhindered operation), is running for the second time in its history, a Complete Course of Instruction - theoretical and practical - of the multifarious work of the Master in Thessaloniki, with the ulterior motive of making His voice heard in the second capital and the potential future foundation of an Omakoio of Thessaloniki.

Some isolated activities are also undertaken by students of the Master in different parts of Greece, such as Komotini, Loutraki of Corinth, Mytilene, etc. where Esoteric Philosophy, Kriya Yoga and certain aspects of Esoteric Therapeutics are presented.

IN THE OMAKOIO OF TRIKALA
THE FOLLOWING DEPARTMENTS
ARE IN OPERATION

A) PUBLICATION - SALES OF BOOKS
WHOLESALE - RETAIL

All the books written and published by the Metaphysicist, Master Nikolaos A. Margioris (189 books in total)
are distributed through the Omakoio of Trikala, Greece.
Please ask for the relevant price list. Also, ask for Ilias L.
Katsiampas' (Nikolaos A. Margioris' student) book *From
the Master's Mouth to the Student's Ear, with a Thorough
Glossary of Sanskrit (Philosophic Dictionary, 400 Words) for
the Students of Yoga.* The following books by the same author are in press a) *A Comprehensive Analytical Dictionary of
Metaphysical Terms* b) *The Systems of Esoteric Therapeutics.*

B) KRIYA YOGA SCHOOL
PSYCHOSOMATIC - THERAPEUTICS

It started operation for the first time in Trikala, in January of 1992. Master of Metaphysics, Yoga and SHIATSU,
N. Margioris revived and established the authentic Kriya
Yoga. He brought back the genuine Kriya from obscu-
rity and made it known again. He taught it in Greece
for the first time in 1981 in the Omakoio of Athens and
he wrote his first book without a Master, *Kriya Yoga - A
Practical Method of Psychosomatic-Therapy.* In this School,
many physical exercises are taught in combination with

rhythmical breathing exercises (Pranayama) so that the Nervous and the Muscular system may become stronger, resulting in health and serenity, as well as the release of the trainee from stress and other psychological disturbances. Kriya is the only path which properly prepares the trainee for his initiation to Concentration (Raja Yoga).

C) RAJA YOGA SCHOOL
MIND ELEVATION FROM CONSCIOUSNESS
TO HYPERCONSCIOUSNESS
It was established and has been in operation in Trikala since December 5, 1991. Instruction is accompanied by Master Nikolaos Margioris' book *RAJA YOGA*. In Raja Yoga, the advanced students are trained only in intellectual exercises aiming to perfect and balance the Mind. The trainee strengthens his will and acquires a larger and clearer understanding of every matter that may occupy him, particularly in Metaphysics. Special exercises in concentration and hyperconcentration only found in Raja Yoga are executed with the purpose of ultimately and gradually reactivating the third and highest Mind function, hyperconsciousness.

Also all the Yoga systems such as Karma, Bhakti, Mantra, Jnani, Kundalini (Tantra) and so on, are taught.

D) SEMINARS OF SHIATSU - SUGGESTION - HYPNOTISM
Every year, many seminars on Therapeutics without medication based on the Japanese technique of SHIATSU

(Namikoshi) are held, while at the same time the ancient Greek method of Massaging (Asclepiaia-Amfiaraeia), of Finger-tapping (Nikolaos A. Margioris' method), of Sleep Therapy (suggestion, hypnotism) and others are taught.

E) SEMINARS AND SPEECHES OF ESOTERIC PHILOSOPHY

In these seminars, topics concerning the entire field of Esoteric Philosophy, Occultism and Mysticism, such as the other Dimensions; the Law of Free Will, of Karma and of Reincarnation; the life and work of great Sage Masters; the Body-Mind-Intellect-Soul-Spirit; the Divine Plan and the Evolution of Creation and so on, are presented.

F) ATMOLIQUEFACTION SCHOOL

SLIMMING

This department of the Omakoio of Trikala operates once or twice a year and its program lasts for about three months. Special physical exercises in combination with the proper breathing exercises (Pranayama - N. Margioris' system) are taught. These are very effective in activating the organism, resulting in perspiration and the burning of fat. At the same time, muscles are strengthened without any mechanical means or medicine.

G) ESOTERIC KEY

STUDIES THROUGH A CORRESPONDENCE COURSE
IN THE FOLLOWING BRANCHES OF ESOTERICISM

1) ASTROLOGY - ASTROSOPHY

2) ESOTERIC PHILOSOPHY

3) SCIENTIFIC SPIRITUALISM

4) HYPNOTISM - ORTHOPSYCHISM

5) ESOTERIC THERAPEUTICS

6) ESOTERIC INITIATION

7) MEDITATION

8) DESYMBOLISM

Those who would like further information and analytical prospectuses about any branch may request them from the OMAKOIO OF TRIKALA, 21 Kefallinias Str., 42131, Trikala, Greece, or call **Mr. Ilias Katsiampas** at the telephone number 0030-24310-75505 or 0030-6974-580768 (mobile).

All the books, essays, journals and correspondence courses by Master Nikolaos A. Margioris, founder of the Omakoio of Athens, are available at the Omakoio of Trikala.

IMPORTANT INFORMATION

All those who would like to be advised about **matters, writings** and **teachings** of **Esoteric-Metaphysical Philosophy, Esoteric Therapeutics** (Shiatsu, Finger-tapping, Static Therapeutics, ancient Greek Asclepean Massage, Sleep Therapy, or otherwise, Hypnotism, etc.), **Yoga Systems** (Kriya, Karma, Gnani, Raja, Bhakti and Kundalini), Gnosticism, Hypnotism-Orthopsychism, Scientific Spiritualism, Esoteric Initiation, Meditation, Esoteric Theology, Astrology-Astrosophy, Desymbolism, etc. may visit our site (www. omakoio.gr) or contact us for more information.

We have at our disposal and readily **available** more than **180 specialized writings** that were a result of the deep experiential spiritual Experience of the modern neo-pythagorean Greek Philosopher and Christocentric mysticist, **Nikolaos A. Margioris** (1913-1933).

On our website (www.omakoio.gr) you can see and order by cash on delivery whichever of his works interests you, our articles, the teaching activities that we offer (lessons, seminars, speeches) as well as our annual programs.

As a GET-TO-KNOW-US OFFER, we provide any interested person with the **Greek-English** 100-page **magazine "New Omakoio"**, which includes all the writings of Nikolaos Margioris as well as other intriguing articles FREE OF CHARGE.

To receive the magazine, you must send us the relevant details concerning where you wish the magazine to be sent.

INTERESTING LINKS WITH INTERVIEWS, ARTICLES AND PRESENTATIONS ABOUT NIKOLAOS MARGIORIS' RARE EXPERIENTIAL PHILOSOPHICAL WORK BY HIS STUDENT ILIAS KATSIAMPAS

http://www.omakoio,gr
http://www.omakoio.gr/indexgrekk.htm

Included in Greek and in English:
Biographical Note of Nikolaos **A. Margioris**, the modern experiential philosopher (1913-1933).

Biographical Note of his student **Ilias Katsiampas** and an informative **Interview** that he gave on the website **Esoterica.gr**.

A series of interesting **Articles by Ilias Katsiampas**.

The interpretation of the word **Omakoio** together with the presentation of the **Neo-pythagorean Practical Philosophical Schools** in Greece.

The **75 writings by Nikolaos Margioris** and the **books** by **Ilias Katsiampas** (summaries and contents for each one separately).

The **49 issues** of the magazine **Omakoio** (summary and contents for each one separately).

The Correspondence course in **8 Branches** of **Esotericism** (Meditation, Hypnotism-Orthopsychism, Scientific Spiritualism, Esoteric Philosophy, Esoteric Initiation, Esoteric Therapeutics, Astrology-Astrosophy, Desymbolism).

Drops of Wisdom derived from the written philosophical work of **Nikolaos Margioris.**

Activities and **Educational Programs** of the Esoteric-Phillosophical Schools (Omakoios) throughout Greece. The following subjects are taught: Kriya Yoga, Karma, Gnani, Bhakti, Raja, Kundalini Yoga, Esoteric Philosophy and Esoteric Therapeutics.

Our site **(www.omakoio.gr)** has been in operation since the end of 1998 and is updated on a regular basis.

http://www.esoterica.gr/podium/interviews/katsiaba/ katsiaba.htm
Interview with Ilias L. Katsiampas on the website of *Esoterica.gr.* It has been posted since Tuesday, 21 May 2002.

http://www.pepfa.gr/06periodiko.hmtl
http://www.pepfa.gr/06periodikoarthro%20katsiam- pa.htm
http://www.esoterica,.gr/articles/contributions/east- ern/katsyoga/katsyoga.htm
An extensive article–proposal–memorandum by **Ilias Katsiampas** toward every person specialized in the scientific method of Yoga and its applications to modern man. Hosted by **PEPFA**, the Panhellenic Association of Graduates of Physical Education in Greece and by **Esoterica.gr.**

It has been posted on the site of PEPFA since June 26th 2004 and on the site of Esoterica.gr since March 3rd 2004.

http://www.esoterica.gr/articles/contributions/altmed/
katsbas/katsbas.htm
Article on *Alternative Therapeutics* by Ilias Katsiampas.
It has been posted since the summer of 2003.

http://www.esoterica.gr/articles/contributions/esoter-
ic/afrmkats/afrmkats.htm
Article by Ilias Katsiampas on *Esoteric Quests and the
Mass Media of Information*.
Metaphysics and the Mass Media of Information. It has
been posted since the end of October of 2003.

http://www.esoterica.gr/articles/contributions/esoter-
ic/katsba2/katsba2.htm
Article by Ilias Katsiampas on the subject of *Metaphysics and Religiousness*.
Posted since the summer of 2003.

http://www.esoterica.gr/guests/omakoio/omakoio.htm
Presentation of the Books of N. Margioris and I. Katsiampas

http://www.esoterica.gr/frlinks.htm
Host to the Activities of the Omakoios of Trikala and
of Thessaloniki

http://www.atlantida.gr/frlinks.htm
Presentation of the website of the Omakoio of Trikala
and of the book *Dravidians, the Ancestors of the Greeks*.

Note: If anyone happens to be interested in publishing and distributing the above books in English or in any other language, he is requested to contact Ilias L. Katsiampas, the writer's student, at the telephone numbers or the e-mail addresses listed below so that he may bring them in touch with Nikolaos Margioris' heirs.

For any further information or clarification, please contact us.

With friendly greetings and esteem
Ilias Katsiampas
(Head of the Omakoios of Trikala and of Thessaloniki)
Tel. & Fax: 24310-75505 or 6974-580768
Website: http://www.omakoio.gr
E-mails: omakoio@omakoio.gr or omakoeio@gmail.com

BIBLIOGRAPHY OF THE WRITER

I) PUBLISHED BOOKS
BY NIKOLAOS A. MARGIORIS
(copyrights belong to his heirs)

1. **Patapios, the Humble Philosopher and Saint from Egypt**, 1st edition in 1970 (156 pages), 2nd edition in 1987 (220 pages), with supplementary and explanatory material, 3rd edition in 2005 (220 pages).

2. **Light in the Dark**, 1st edition in 1975 (300 pages), 2nd edition in 1987 (429 pages) with supplementary and explanatory material, 3rd edition in 2005 (429 pages).

3. **Theurgy Teaches the Eternal Way of the Soul**, 1st edition in 1975 (318 pages), 2nd edition in 1987 (408 pages), with supplementary and explanatory material.

4. **The Other View of Erich Von Daniken's Dogma**, 1st edition in 1976 (318 pages), 2nd edition in 1994 (372 pages), with supplementary and explanatory material. ISBN: 960-7484-00-2.

5. **The Secret of Hatha Yoga**, 1st edition in 1976 (111 pages), 2nd edition in 1977 (155 pages). ISBN: 960-7484-04-5.

6. **Pythagorean Arithmosophy**, 1st edition in 1977 (168 pages), 2nd edition in 1987 (271 pages), 3rd edition in 1993 (276 pages) with supplementary and explanatory material, 4th edition in 2000 (276 pages), 5th edition in 2004 (282 pages). ISBN: 960-7152-06-09.

7. **The Eleusinian Mysteries**, 1st edition in 1978 (99

pages), 2nd edition in 1987 (159 pages), 3rd edition in 1993 (178 pages) with supplementary and explanatory material, 4th edition in 1999 (183 pages). ISBN: 960-7152-11-5.

8. **The Last Day of Socrates**, 1st edition in 1978 (111 pages), 2nd edition in 1988 (152 pages), with supplementary and explanatory material.

9. **The Pharaohs Akhenaten and Tutankhamun**, 1st edition in 1978 (151 pages), 2nd edition in 1991 (311 pages), with supplementary and explanatory material. ISBN: 960-7152-00-X.

10. **The Birth and Death of the Worlds and the Beings (matter-antimatter-hypermatter, universe-antiuniverse-hyperuniverse)**, 1st edition in 1979 (195 pages), 2nd edition in 1990 (323 pages), with supplementary and explanatory material, 3rd edition in 2009 (323 pages). ISBN: 960-85024-5-4.

11. **Dravidians, the Ancestors of the Greeks (Synopsis) in English**, 1st edition in 1979 (45 pages).

12. **The Reign of Minos, the Great King of Crete**, 1st edition in 1979 (88 pages), 2nd edition in 1997 (105 pages). ISBN: 960-7484-06-1.

13. **Dravidians, the Ancestors of Greeks**, 1st edition in 1979 (88 pages), 2nd edition in 1989 (143 pages), with supplementary and explanatory material, 3rd edition in 1996 (167 pages), 4th edition in 2004 (166 pages).

14. **Eastern and Western White and Black Magic**, 1st edition in 1979 (134 pages),

15. **White Magic**, 2nd edition in 1992 (227 pages) with

supplementary and explanatory material. ISBN: 960-7152-03-4.

16. **Barefoot They Dance on Fire (Anastenaria)**, 1st edition in 1980 (95 pages).

17. **Post-Mortem Life (or Life after Death)**, 1st edition in 1982 (256 pages), 2nd edition in 1993 (262 pages), 3rd edition in 2010 (262 pages). ISBN: 960-7152-09-3.

18. **Raja Yoga**, 1st edition in 1983 (208 pages).

19. **The Two-Volume Metaphysical Encyclopaedia**, 1st edition in 1985/86 (Volume A, 443 pages, Volume B, 752 pages).

20. **Kriya Yoga – A Practical Method of Psychosomatic Therapy**, 1st edition in 1988 (357 pages), 2nd edition in 2000 (359 pages).

21. **The Desymbolism of Greek Mythology**, 1st edition in 1988 (521 pages), 2nd edition in 2002 (562 pages).

22. **The Three-Dimensional and Four-Dimensional World**, 1st edition in 1989 (214 pages), 2nd edition in 2007 (222 pages). ISBN: 960-85024-3-8.

23. **Mystical Teachings, Volume A**, 1st edition in 1991 (346 pages). ISBN: 960-85024-1-1 SET 960-85024-7-0.

24. **Karma. The Law of Retributive Justice**, 1st edition in 1989 (373 pages), 2nd edition in 1996 (373 pages), 3rd edition in 2009 (373 pages). ISBN: 960-85024-0-3.

25. **Reincarnation**, 1st edition in 1990 (286 pages), 2nd edition in 2009 (286 pages). ISBN: 960-85024-4-6.

26. **The Chiroplastic Therapeutics of SHIATSU, Volume A**, 1st edition in 1990 (533 pages). ISBN: 960-85024-6-2.

27. **Psychotherapeutics without Medication,** 1st edition in 1991 (325 pages). ISBN: 960-85024-8-9.

28. **Mysticism. Christocentric and Christocratic Mysticism,** 1st edition in 1991 (331 pages). ISBN: 960-85024-9-7.

29. **Occultism (Occultology), Volume A,** 1st edition in 1991 (391 pages). ISBN: 960-7152-01-8, 960-7152-02-6.

30. **Occultism (Occultology), Volume B,** 1st edition in 1992 (428 pages). ISBN: 960-7152-01-8, T.2. 960-7152-04-2.

31. **The Chiroplastic Therapeutics of SHIATSU, Volume B,** 1st edition in 1993 (395 pages). ISBN: SET 960-7152-07-7, 960-7152-08-5.

32. **Mystical Teachings, Volume B,** 1st edition in 1993 (388 pages). ISBN: SET 960-85024-7-0, 960-7152-05-0.

33. **Mystical Teachings, Volume C,** 1st edition in 1994 (379 pages). ISBN: SET 960-85024-7-0, 960-7152-10-7.

34. **The Chiroplastic Therapeutics of SHIATSU, Volume C,** 1st edition in 1993 (255 pages).

35. **Occultism (Occultology), Volume C,** 1st edition in 1997, 103 pages. ISBN: 960-7484-05-3.

II) ESSAYS BY NIKOLAOS. A. MARGIORIS

1. SCHOOL OF ASCLEPEANS - HYPNOTHERAPISTS
2. CARL VON REICHENBACH
3. SCHOOL OF AESKLEPIANS - SPIRITUAL THERAPISTS
   THEOPHRASTUS PARACELSUS
4. MAGNETOTHERAPY
5. ASCLEPIAIA AND AMFIARAEIA
6. THE THERAPY FROM BEFORE TIME
7. THE CELL AND LIFE MYSTERY
8. ECTOPLASM
9. ESSENES
10. APPARITIONS OF IDOLS OF LIVING PEOPLE
11. ANASTENARIA
12. CREATION OF THE WORLDS
13. MYSTICISM
14. DRAVIDIANS, THE FIRST GREEKS OF THE AEGEAN
    SEA
15. THE CONTROL OF VIBRATIONS
16. WHAT IS ESOTERICISM?
17. THE HOLY SCROLLS OF THE ESSENE RULES
18. EROS AND LOVE
19. PROPER NUTRITION, PROPER DIET, WEIGHT LOSS
20. THERAPEUTICS WITHOUT MEDICATION
21. THERAPEUTICS THROUGH HYPNOTISM
22. THERAPY OF PSYCHOPATHY

23. SHIATSU. THERAPEUTIC METHOD TWO VOLUMES
(1st seminar)

24. SHIATSU. THERAPEUTIC METHOD TWO VOLUMES
(2nd seminar)

25. SHIATSU. THERAPEUTUC METHOD TWO VOLUMES
(3rd seminar)

26. SHIATSU. THERAPEUTIC METHOD TWO VOLUMES
(4th seminar)

27. SHIATSU. THERAPEUTIC METHOD TWO VOLUMES
(5th seminar)

28. SHIATSU. THERAPEUTIC METHOD ONE VOLUME (6th
seminar)

29. SHIATSU. THERAPEUTIC METHOD ONE VOLUME (7th
seminar)

30. SHIATSU. THERAPEUTIC METHOD ONE VOLUME (8th
seminar)

31. SHIATSU. THERAPEUTIC METHOD ONE VOLUME (9th
seminar)

32. SHIATSU. THERAPEUTIC METHOD ONE VOLUME
(10th seminar)

33. SHIATSU. THERAPEUTIC METHOD ONE VOLUME
(11th seminar)

III) OMAKOIO JOURNAL
BY NIKOLAOS A. MARGIORIS (49 issues)

The best **metaphysical** *and* **occultist magazine** of our country. **Its every article** *is a* **revelation. Its every page** is an **enlightenment.** It contains **well-documented** *and* **rare metaphysical analyses** on plenty of esoteric matters. It comes in hexads. It was in circulation for **8 years (1977-1985)** in bimonthly publications. The first issue is number 2 and the last is number 49 (total of pages: 1658). There are 8 hexads at **25.00€** per hexad.

IV) ESOTERIC KEY
BY NIKOLAOS A. MARGIORIS

Esotericism and **Metaphysics** are presented in complete form in their practical application and they give the student the **KEY OF KNOWLEDGE.**

Seven Branches *of* **Esotericism**, with **thirty** or **thirty-three** treatises of lessons. Every Branch contains approximately ten or eleven triads or thirty to thirty-three chapters – lessons. See summaries and contents for every branch separately on our site: www.omakoio.gr

Every lesson – triad costs **15.00 Euro. Enrolment** is a one-time fee of **10.00 Euro.** Ask for informative printed enrolment forms for the Esoteric Key branches of study by correspondence course.

The Branches are the following:

1) MEDITATION
2) HYPNOTISM - ORTHOPSYCHISM
3) SCIENTIFIC SPIRITUALISM
4) ESOTERIC PHILOSOPHY
5) ESOTERIC INITIATION
6) ASTROLOGY - ASTROSOPHY
7) ESOTERIC THERAPEUTICS
8) DESYMBOLISM

Nikolaos Margioris' books that are translated into English, or that are currently in the process of being translated, are the following:

1) Dravidians, the Ancestors of the Greeks (translated, in a book), **2) Life After Death** (translated), **3) The Birth and Death of the Worlds and the Beings** (matter, antimatter, hypermatter, universe, antiuniverse, hyperuniverse) (in the process of being translated), **4) Kriya Yoga** (translated) and **5) Raja Yoga** (translated).

BOOKS BY ILIAS L. KATSIAMPAS
(N. MARGIORIS' STUDENT) OMAKOIOS
OF TRIKALA AND OF THESSALONIKI, GREECE
(AND YOGA ACADEMY
OF NIKOLAOS MARGIORIS – OMAKOIO)

My own books (**Ilias Katsiampas**, student of **Master N. Margioris**) that relate directly to Margioris' work, translated into English, are the following:

1) **10-year Anniversary of the Establishment of the Omakoio of Athens by Master N. A. Margioris.** A bilingual **Greek-English 1999 edition** in an A4 thermal-bound edition, the Greek text consisting of 34 pages and the English text of 33 pages.

2) **A Full and Most Analytical Dictionary – Guide of Metaphysical Meanings**, in press.

3) **Asclepean Art and the Systems of Esoteric Therapeutics**, in press.

4) **Bilingual Greek-English Magazine "New Omakoio"**, size A4, 1st issue, of 100 pages. All the 189 writings of Master Nikolaos Margioris are included in Greek and in English, with a photo of the cover, summaries and contents for each one separately, esoteric articles and the Schools-Omakoios that function in Greece.

5) **Collection of Articles – Advice & Interviews** of Ilias L. Katsiampas, 1st edition in an A4 thermal-bound edition. October 2004. First Reward from the International Union (Company) Greek Man of Letters (DEEL).

6) **Esoteric and Spiritual Experiences of Master Nikolaos A. Margioris.** A bilingual **Greek-English edition** in an A4 thermal-bound edition. 1st edition 2004.

7) **From Deep Metaphysical Correspondence.** In Greek, 1st edition 2007, 400 pages.

8) **From the Master's Mouth to the Student's Ear, with a thorough glossary of Sanskrit (philosophic dictionary, 400 words) for the students of Yoga,** 1st edition 1995 (270 pages), dimensions 24X17, ISBN: 960-85735-0-5. In the Greek language, it is available in book form. The English translation is also available in an A4 thermal-bound edition.

9) **Handbook – Guide for Staff and Instructors of Esotericism According to Master Nikolaos A. Margioris'** **Work.** It exists **in Greek** in an A4 thermal-bound edition (202 pages), 1st edition 2003 and **in English** as a separate edition (206 pages), **only for the members of the Omakoios.**

10) **Inauguration of the Omakoio of Lamia by Master N. A. Margioris.** A bilingual **Greek-English 2000 edition** in an A4 thermal-bound edition, the Greek

text consisting of 36 pages and the English text of 22 pages.

11) **Inauguration of the Omakoio of Trikala by Master N. A. Margioris.** A bilingual **Greek-English 1999 edition** in an A4 thermal-bound edition, the Greek text consisting of 57 pages and the English text of 38 pages.

12) **Meditation and Mysticism, Raja and Kundalini Yoga (Theory and Practice)**, in press.

13) **Plagues and Provocations of our Time. The Metaphysical View.** In press.

14) **Prayer Book and Poems of Master Nikolaos A. Margioris.** A bilingual **Greek-English edition.** In book form. 1st edition 2004. First Reward from the International Union (Company) Greek Man of Letters (DEEL).

15) **The Apocalypse of John as Explained by Master Nikolaos A. Margioris** (A bilingual Greek-English edition, supervised and with extensive analytical annotations by his student, Ilias L. Katsiampas), 1st edition 1999, ISBN: 960-85735-1-3. Second Award from the International Union (Company) Greek Man of letters (DEEL).

16) **The Mystery of Death and the Post-Mortem Course of the Soul.** In press.

17) **The Question of Aliens.** In press.

Information
Ilias Katsiampas
21 Kefallinias str., 42131 Trikala, Greece
Tel. and Fax 0030-24310-75505
or mobile: 0030-6974-580768
Website: http://www.omakoio.gr
or https://omakoio.blogspot.com
E-mails: omakoio@omakoio.gr
or omakoeio@gmail.com

PRESENTATIONS ON YOUTUBE
AND ON FACEBOOK OF 189 WRITINGS
OF MODERN GREEK MYSTIC
NIKOLAOS A. MARGIORIS (1913-1993)
AND OF 14 BOOKS OF HIS STUDENT
ILIAS KATSIAMPAS

-With English Subtitles-

IN ENGLISH (With English Subtitles)
-VIDEO PRESENTATION IN ENGLISH OF 35
BOOKS OF MODERN GREEK MYSTIC NIKOLAOS
A. MARGIORIS (1913-1993).
With English Subtitles. TIME: 61 MINUTES.
http://youtu.be/GUbJ3RbhpIQ
https://www.youtube.com/watch?v=GUbJ3RbhpIQ&feature=youtu.be

-VIDEO OF THE INAUGURATION OF THE NEOPY-
THAGOREAN SCHOOL OMAKOIO OF TRIKALA BY
GREEK SPIRITUAL MASTER NIKOLAOS A. MAR-
GIORIS THAT TOOK PLACE ON SATURDAY, JAN-
UARY 18th 1992, 20.00 Hrs. With English Subtitles.
1st Part of VIDEO (Duration: 2:02:44)
http://youtu.be/KU3JalIc5HI or
https://www.youtube.com/watch?v=KU3JalIc5HI&feature=youtu.be

-VIDEO OF THE INAUGURATION OF THE NEOPY-THAGOREAN SCHOOL OMAKOIO OF TRIKALA BY GREEK SPIRITUAL MASTER NIKOLAOS A. MARGIORIS THAT TOOK PLACE ON SATURDAY, JANUARY 19th 1992, 20.00 Hrs. With English Subtitles.
2nd Part of VIDEO (Duration: 1:26:15)
http://youtu.be/YR3I-WqVawI or
https://www.youtube.com/watch?v=YR3I-WqVawI&feature=youtu.be

-VIDEO OF THE CELEBRATION OF THE 10 YEARS (1976-1986) SINCE THE FOUNDATION OF THE OMAKOIO OF ATHENS BY MASTER NIKOLAOS A. MARGIORIS, FRIDAY, NOVEMBER 27th, 1987, 21:00. With English Subtitles.
-AND BANQUET AND SPEECH AT THE GOLDEN AGE HOTEL, ATHENS, WITH AN AWARD OF HONORARY MEDALS BY MASTER NIKOLAOS A. MARGIORIS TO HIS STUDENTS, JULY 1987. Video Duration: 2h & 7min.
With English Subtitles.
http://youtu.be/D79MIXeDgaE
https://www.youtube.com/watch?v=D79MIXeDgaE&feature=youtu.be

Produced and translated into English by Ilias Katsiampas

SPEECH N. MARGIORIS IN HOUSE OF KROMVAS WITH SUBS IN ENGLISH
Athens 12-3-1988. Video Duration: 1h & 34 min.
https://www.youtube.com/watch?v=luWXYyM36l8

Produced by Ilias Katsiampas and translated into English by Anna Giavasi. Editing: Ilias Katsiampas, Anna Giavasi, Niki Foufa, Mprenta Kathesides and Kimonas Petrocheilos.

PAGES ON FACEBOOK:

NIKOLAOS A. MARGIORIS A GREEK SPIRITUAL
MASTER (A MODERN SPIRITUAL FIGURE)
https://www.facebook.com/pages/NIKOLAOS-A-MAR-
GIORIS-A-MODERN-GREEK-SPIRITUAL-FORM/110183
632346517?ref=bookmarks

GROUPS ON FACEBOOK

**YOGA ACADEMY OF NIKOLAOS MARGIORIS –
OMAKOEIO**
https://www.facebook.com/groups/848311315181471/

**ESOTERICISM FOR ALL - GROUP AND FRIENDS
OF NIKOLAOS A. MARGIORIS**
https://www.facebook.com/groups/310048335902/

**2012-2014 ARRIVAL OR INVASION OF EXTRA-
TERRESTRIALS (ALIENS)?**
https://www.facebook.com/pages/2012-2014-AR-
RIVAL-OR-INVASION-EXTRATERRESTRIAL-AL-
IENS/223243041058772?fref=ts

**PROFILE FACEBOOK ILIAS KATSIAMPAS AD-
MINISTRATOR OF PAGES-GROUPS**
https://www.facebook.com/ilias.katsiampas

**SECOND PROFILE FACEBOOK OF ILIAS KATSI-
AMPAS ADMINISTRATOR OF PAGES-GROUPS**
https://www.facebook.com/ekatsiampas?fref=ts

SUMMARY OF THE WORK

After many years of thorough research, investigation and study, we discovered that there is a big void concerning the transcription of small or great esoteric experiences of spiritual Masters.

And this void is more apparent when we refer to the **revelatory works** that touch upon the **mystical truth** and its rendition in **physical form** (oral and particularly written).

In view of the fact that existing written records of spiritual experiences are few, extremely terse, hard to understand or unconnected with each other – and for the most part of little esoteric or spiritual depth – we thought that it would be useful to provide examples of **spiritual occurrences** found in the **hyperconscious experiences** of our Master **Nikolaos A. Margioris** that concern all of humanity and the course of its evolution which, through its gradual self-perfection, is ultimately guided towards them.

Because descriptions of such **profound spiritual experiences** (apart from or along with the presence of occult experiences) are few and far between, especially those accompanied by a rich analysis and an extensive unrivalled description, we deemed it imperative to collect them and to record them for everyone's benefit.

Additionally, it is with certainty that we believe that

prominence can and should be given, whenever possible, to the **unwavering STANDARDS leading** towards the **ONE hyperconscious path of ascension** and **true spiritual ENLIGHTENMENT** as well as to the everlasting **qualities of THEOSIS** which may be detected or at least mentioned. Because of this certainty, we make these highly valuable and interesting spiritual experiences public for the first time.